e follow

# Who Is Artie Shaw...
## and why is he following me?

### by
### Ferdie Pacheco

authorHOUSE™

*1663 Liberty Drive, Suite 200*
*Bloomington, Indiana 47403*
*(800) 839-8640*
*www.AuthorHouse.com*

First published by AuthorHouse 07/06/05

ISBN: 1-4208-3805-9 (e)
ISBN: 1-4208-3804-0 (sc)

Printed in the United States of America
Bloomington, Indiana

This book is printed on acid-free paper.

# Table of Contents

# Forward

I've met a lot of people in my life from Charles Lindbergh and Charlie Chaplin to Scott Fitzgerald and John Steinbeck, Marlon Brando and Muhammad Ali. If I had to pick the single most unequal I'd have to nominate Dr. Ferdie Pacheco.

People count themselves blessed when they're gifted with a talent. So what do you say to Pacheco the ghetto doctor who became a corner man for Muhammad Ali wrote excellent books on boxing and became a boxing announcer, that's only the beginning. A distinguished painter, he's also a novelist, a war historian, and what I find most appealing about Ferdie is his tireless creative enthusiasm.

Now he brings those gifts to his unique book on the unique Artie Shaw. He's a legendary white jazz clarinetist of the 40's and 50's, Artie Shaw deserving of a whole bookshelf to himself. But somehow Dr. Pacheco whose fascination with the musical art of Artie Shaw began when he was still a schoolboy, has managed to capture not just the artistry but the quirky character of Artie Shaw in this short, pithy, entertaining book. You get two for the price of one here because as clearly as Artie Shaw's full-palette persona comes through, so does Renaissance Man's Dr. Ferdie Pacheco. Begin the Beguine...

Budd Schulberg

# The Big Betrayal: A Kid's View

Have you ever been betrayed by a hero you have cherished as a boy? It hurt, you know?

Since 1937 I have been in love with a musical sound, a song, an arrangement, and, above all an unusual melodic, lyrical, sensual clarinet. My friend Henry Angulo, the athlete hero of our block, one summer got so worked up over the sound of that band that he stopped playing baseball at Cuscaden Park, and began practicing the clarinet six, sometimes eight hours a day. Henry's father, Dr. Ismail Angulo, was our family doctor, and in the days of the Depression, few people I knew could afford to buy a Selmer clarinet for their teenage son. When Henry demonstrated a real talent and fierce determination, Dr. Angulo furnished him with a Spanish clarinet master teacher. He knew nothing of jazz, but acknowledged Artie Shaw was the best clarinetist.

That summer of 1937 was memorable. Henry would strip down to his BVDs and white undershirt place an electric fan at his feet, sit down after lunch, and not get up until supper. Such determination I never imagined anyone had. Henry, an All-State football player exhibited that grit on a football field, but that was sports, playing ball. That wasn't hard work that was fun. Blowing into a clarinet and getting uncertain results was definitely *not* fun. Yet Henry stuck to it. Squeaks and squacks, which the harsh Spanish taskmaster called *Gallos,* or "Roosters," did not discourage the persistent Henry.

If Henry had had the benefit of Artie Shaw's answer to an English journalist's question about playing the clarinet for fun, he would have learned Shaw's explanation, "What makes you think blowing into a block of wood, exerting your lungs, your lips, your tongue and pharynx, working your fingers is fun? That is hard work, man. Once I was the best clarinetist in the world. Now, if I tried to play like I used to I'd be a horrible failure. I can't do it any more. I don't want to make a sound. I want to play like I used to play. Do you think that could be considered fun?"

As far as I was concerned, from my comfortable vantage point on the bed, surrounded by Dr. Angulo's weekly magazines, *Life, Look, Time, Colliers, Saturday Evening Post,* what Henry was doing was torture. Hard work with meager results. Fun didn't enter into it.

Our obsession with Artie Shaw began when someone told me about the number one record in America. My father, a druggist, brought home a new big Philco Console radio. I was crestfallen because it had no phonograph attached. The salvation lay at Kress' Five and Dime, where you could buy a small triangular phonograph to attach to the big radio. It cost $8.00, and my father bought it grudgingly.

The one problem which arose immediately was a lack of records. Our house had a few Caruso records, and a few Toscanini conducting the NBC Symphony. So, when I heard of this phenomenal record, I started washing cars at a dime a car, and when I had 35¢, I marched down to Woolworth's record counter. I had written the name of the record on my school paper and I asked, "'Begin the Beguine,' by Artie Shaw on Bluebird, please."

The beautiful blue-eyed girl smiled at me and said, "You're cute," to get me to blush which I, of course, did. She handed me the shiny disc. I raced home and played it.

Oh, the first time anyone hears Shaw solo on "Begin the Beguine" is as memorable as a first kiss. I played it over and over and over. My old grandmother said, "Isn't there another side to that?"

I flipped it over. It had a comic side with Tony Pastor singing "Indian Love Call." It was nice but no match for "Begin the Beguine." My grandmother sniffed, "I like the 'Love Call' better."

I ran down to Henry's house. His father had a gigantic RCA Victor, with push buttons, a record changer, and four speakers in a huge mahogany case. Mysteriously, it had a big green eye that changed according to the music. It was hypnotic.

Henry swears it was that day that he made up his mind to play clarinet like Artie Shaw. Poor Henry, the entire musical world was trying to play clarinet like Artie Shaw and no one was able to match him, not even Benny Goodman.

In retrospect I can see clearly, and justify, why I became a 10 year-old Artie Shaw groupie. Between my clarinetist pal Henry and I we bought every record that Artie Shaw made. The 78's then LP 33 1/3's came out. We bought every Artie Shaw LP issued. Then they went to tape. We bought every tape Artie Shaw made. And now, when I am 74 years old, and Shaw is 91, he has reissued five CDs with every Artie Shaw record ever made. Can you figure out how many times I bought "Begin the Beguine"?

What I am bemusedly looking at is the journey a little boy of 10 took to reach to 74, and still find Artie Shaw's "Begin the Beguine" the finest most pleasurable listening experience in his 10,000 record jazz collection. Is it a sickness?

As to the hobby I fell into, by chance, I have no coherent explanation other than this. Tampa was a small isolated town. The newspapers were purely for local news. National news, especially about the entertainment business, was slim. We were crazy to read about our heroes, in this case, Artie Shaw. So we began almost involuntarily to seek out Artie Shaw mentions. If a new nonfiction book came out, I went directly to the index. Usually there was a Shaw, George Bernard, hardly ever Shaw, Artie.

We had no hope of hearing the band live, for band remotes from hotels and nightclubs did not exist in Tampa. The only program featuring live big bands was from Frank Daly's Meadowbrook, a full hour on Saturdays, and I never missed a program yet I never once heard Artie Shaw.

So, imagine if you can the thirst to know about your hero which goes unsatiated year after year. Once in awhile, a major break. Artie Shaw makes *Dancing Coed* with several band numbers. A major Shaw hit was *Second Chorus* (1940) with Fred Astaire and Paulette Goddard. Not only did Shaw have a few scenes where he talked (so that's what Shaw sounds like) but he got to play "Concerto for Clarinet" which was kind of his answer to Benny Goodman's "Sing, Sing, Sing." We went to see that picture every day. Today I have that VCR in my file.

Call it a peculiarity. Call it a habit. Call it an obsession. I could not stop keeping track of Artie Shaw. Artie Shaw? An idol of a lifetime? Come on. Get serious.

Yes, embarrassing as that may sound, I became a secret gatherer of Artie Shaw minutia. Everyone seemed to have an Artie Shaw story. He was hilarious in his self obsessed eccentricity. I continued to snip out clippings about Artie Shaw. Soon, I had drawers full of clippings. Why didn't he plummet from sight?

"Begin the Beguine," "Frenesi," "Stardust," "Dancing in the Dark," "Summit Ridge Drive," "Cross Your Heart" and many other recordings of his fabulous band of 1938 to 1948 kept being reissued. They sold again, like hot cakes. More press, more interviews. *That's why.*

Shaw was always loud in his criticism of the music business and was quoted in a jazz magazine as saying, "I love the music part, but it's not the music-music I loath. I hate the business-business. It's not about music. One owner, when I was starting out, yelled at me one night as I was defending our music.

"Music? Go get stuffed. I don't care if you get up there and the whole band takes a shit in unison. If people pay me many dollars to see you take a shit then that is what I want. These people paid to dance, that is what I want."

Shaw went on to say, the man was heavy into polkas and waltzes, and told Shaw to aim to have a band like Lawrence Welk or Russ Morgan.

Shaw walked. He was always walking away. When his "hot, loud" band was at the height of its popularity Shaw found himself, at

26, making $26,000 a week. Average salaries in Depression America were at $20 to $30 a week! Shaw walked out in the middle of his set. This is where Artie Shaw first insinuated himself into my life.

My buddy Henry Angulo and I idolized Artie Shaw. Henry did everything I wanted to do but couldn't. He played all sports, and was always first string. He even had colleges lined up to recruit him. We became jazz addicts and read all we could and talked to real musicians the rare time we could find any. We'd study each issue of the magazines, Downbeat or Metronome.

"Hey Henry!" I would come into the room where Henry was sweating over a difficult piece of music, "Did you hear? Cootie Williams has left Duke Ellington's band and joined Benny (I always used the familiar for Benny Goodman, but kept a respectful Artie Shaw for Shaw)."

"Well, he needs to have a great horn man to replace Harry James, who is going to form a band, and Ziggy Elman who's going to Dorsey." Henry pursed his lips still fingering the clarinet, giving it his deepest thought (his thought meant a lot to me because Henry was a musician).

"Um. Cootie is a powerhouse all right, but he's been with a black band so long, can he fit and play white jazz?"

"You got a point."

"But Henry, Jazz ain't got no color. Why blacks invented it. Look at Louis Armstrong, Ellington, Fletcher Henderson and Count Basie?"

Henry gave me a withering stare. After all I wasn't no musician!

"But Goodman and Shaw perfected it!"

"Hm." I said, and stuck my head into a new *Life* magazine, properly chastised. Henry knew; he was a musician.

So it was with unbridled joy that I burst into his lesson with the sour old Spanish clarinet professor and yelled, "Henry! He's coming here! Coming to Tampa! Artie Shaw is coming to the Park Theater, Friday, Saturday, and Sunday."

"We'll go to all 3 days," says Henry, whose father is a doctor, and could afford it. I started to wash cars. I meant to attend all three days.

So Friday, for the first show at noon Henry and I are sitting in the first row waiting for the down beat on "Nightmare" Artie Shaw's theme song. The tom-toms start, heavy chords, wailing blues Saxes and…and… no Artie Shaw clarinet. What? We look at each other. A tenor sax play's Artie's part. What? Tony Pastor? Deep dissatisfaction starts in my gut. An electric shock jolted my brain. Something is wrong.

The curtain goes up, and an officious looking theater manager, in a bow tie, dragging in a microphone came center stage.

"We're sorry folks but Artie Shaw has vanished! He disappeared and everyone is looking for him. If you want your money back…"

He doesn't get to finish the statement before the entire theater gets up and leaves. Henry and I stumble home numb with disappointment. No Artie Shaw.

"Benny Goodman wouldn't have done that!" says Henry, switching allegiance in mid disappearance.

"Benny Goodman isn't married to Ava Gardner," I say doggedly defending my idol Artie Shaw, but let me tell you, it was years before I could forgive Artie Shaw for his grievous betrayal. Years! And had I met him face to face anytime before he was 60 I'd have popped him in the mouth!

That betrayal lasted 60 years. But that was the longest most painful walk home from the Park Theater. Henry took the streetcar. He was a doctor's son. He had a nickel.

It was lonely. The sun was high in the sky beating down on my head. Tears welled up in my eyes, and as I hit Florida Avenue, about halfway home, tears started streaming down my cheek. I was sobbing openly.

I've been left standing after long affairs by beautiful ladies, have been divorced twice by two gorgeous girls, but I learned the meaning of heartbreak when Artie Shaw broke my heart.

Hell, if I had known enough to play a guitar and write a little music, I'd have written a number one hill-billy ditty. "I left my heart at the Park Theater."

See, at 13, my life was okay until then. I never had anything to cry about. I had an idyllic home life. Mom and Dad, widowed grandmother and spinster aunt and a bachelor uncle named Ferdie. They all loved me. I loved everybody. My heart had never been tested before; life was very good to me for 13 years.

It was forty years later before *I* witnessed another such a complete first case of heartbreak. I was completely involved with my beautiful six-year old daughter. She was a gorgeous copy of my wife Luisita. She watched TV seated between us on the bed until time to go to her room. Then I had initiated a ritual of going to the kitchen and getting her a few cookies and a glass of milk, and tucking her in her bed.

This night I was deep into a TV drama and wanted to wait until it was over. She whined and cried softly which was very unusual. Tina never cried. Finally, in exasperation, I said, "Oh, go on to the kitchen and get the cookies and milk by yourself. You're old enough now."

At that she set up a wail and a racket that would not stop. I was shocked. "What's the matter, Tina? You've never cried like this since you were born."

She gulped to a stop and said in a clear voice, her hands on her hips, her lips trembling, "Up to now, everything has been all right around here..."

Somehow, the long walk served to clear my mind and my sinuses. I was still a loyal fan. "There must have been a reason for Artie Shaw to disappear."

How was I to know it would take 63 years to get the answer.

The solution to this bitter chapter in the Artie Shaw story came in a most unusual way. Nothing is ever simple with Artie Shaw.

I sat down to enjoy the *Sunday N.Y. Times* Entertainment Section and was shocked to see the 93-year old face of Artie Shaw splattered across the front page. What?

Shaw, it turns out was re-issuing a 5-CD volume of his biggest hits of all his bands. In addition to which he'd written the liner notes. He was still front page in the *N.Y.Times.*

Of course I went to the computer and bought six of them to distribute to various friends. My wife noticed he had listed his home address and she did an unusual thing.

Since I turned 70, I have dreamed perfect short stories, with great O'Henry punch lines. I have 50 done. I'm saving them for a book and/or TV series.

One night I dreamed a perfect story about an old KGB executioner who is seated in his dacha waiting to be killed. Two men come and a friendly conversation ensues. They are in an awe of the legendary hit man.

Finally he asks a favor. He wants to be shot but while listening to his favorite record he first heard when he was a political commissar for the International Brigades in Spain in 1937, and had to shoot an officer from New York. He plays Shaw's "Begin the Beguine." The men are impressed. Still, they don't really know what a clarinet is, much less when he hits a high note.

"Let me play it again," he says. "Did that record sound scratchy to you?"

"Yes, but considering that the phonograph is from 1910..."

"No, no. It's the needle. It has to be changed every five plays. Do you mind if I change it?"

"Of course not."

Whereupon the old warrior opens a drawer, pulls out a Luger and shoots both men between the eyes.

Then the old man looks at the camera (in this case, me) and says, "Isn't it ironic, Shaw only had one hit, and I've had 356?"

End of dream, which I named "The KGB and Artie Shaw."

Unbeknownst to me my wife mailed it to Artie Shaw at his home. Here's the story.

# Artie Shaw and the KGB

Alex Karov poured a cupful of hot tea and sat heavily in an easy chair facing the door. In his eightieth year, he was no longer the spry lion that he had been. His life had been spent hunting men and eliminating them, and was so good at it that Stalin, Kruschev and the lot that followed all made sure his identity was unknown. Stalin had handpicked Alex himself for three qualities; 1. He never missed, 2. He was ruthless and, 3. He never asked questions. Stalin came to rely on him.

But now, in the year 2000, his country had fallen apart. Communism was no longer en vogue. Reformers were poring over all the old documents, sifting out crimes, filling in the mysteries of the past century. Alex knew that when his astounding record of assassinations was made known, the hum and cry for his neck would be deafening.

"So what?" he thought. "I live a boring life in this lonely dacha by the great river, reliving old hits, talking to ghosts, watching old films of the Great War over and over."

World War II was the highlight of his life and it filled him the pride to watch the old films of Stalingrad and Krakow. When he was feeling really mellow he hauled out the old 16-mm projector and ran the films of his days with the International Brigade, when he had been Walter's executioner. Those were the days!

Now he waited for "them" to come. Would it be one man? Or a group? Or would they give him the respect he deserved and permit him to kill himself? What in the hell did it matter? He was 80, ready to go. Time to reunite with hose hundreds of men he had killed. What would life and death be like? He was dying to know.

Toward suppertime, he heard a car pull up in the drive. Two door slams told him he would not be taken by one man. Perhaps they still feared him. Without knocking, they came in. Two of them, one big guy – a policeman type – and one small man – a KGB interrogator type. Alex smiled, waved them to enter and offered tea or vodka.

"Very good. Now go sit in the car. This won't take long," Alex said and poured some hot tea for himself. The two men sat facing one another, the interrogator looked sad and bothered.

"I am a great admirer of your work," he began. "I read the filed – all of them. You were an officer in the Civil War at 14, a Major by 16 and a Colonel by the time you were 18."

"Ah, records lie. The Civil War was a bloody mess. I rose in rank simply because I outlived my buddies. If it had lasted one more month I'd have been a General, and when Comrade Stalin came into power, after we killed Comrade Lenin, he would have taken me out and shot me. Too much success too soon made a person ambitious and Comrade Stalin had a nose for ambitious generals."

"You killed Lenin. That is not in the records."

Alex shrugged as if it didn't matter to him one whit whether this assassin believed him or not.

"Records lie. Did you really think Stalin would leave a notation of Lenin's death?"

"But Lenin, he was our God!"

"That is why Stalin killed him. In Comrade Stalin's world there was only room for on God, and that God was Joseph Stalin."

"How did you earn your spurs?" The KGB man pressed on.

"My spurs?" Alex laughed loudly. "God, I haven't heard that phrase since the Great War. My spurs, as you put it, turned out to be the delicate task of removing Stalin's wife. She was proving embarrassing. It didn't take much. He appreciated my discretion. He could have had me eliminated to insure secrecy. Instead, he fell in love with me. I did not speak to him at all. He called, I answered, he gave me a name on a piece of paper, or a list of names – never more than 10 – and I would salute and leave.

"I went straight to the doomed man's dacha, that very night sometimes, and shot him as soon as he appeared. No conversation, no pleas, explanations or goodbyes. Sometimes, his wife was with him, I shot her, too. Such was my latitude. As soon as I completed my mission, I literally ran to Comrade Stalin's apartments and said only one thing, 'Mission Accomplished.' Refusing a drink of vodka or a piece of fruit, I saluted, about-faced and got out from in front of the mouth of the cannon as soon as I could.

"Stalin loved me! He bragged to Berea that I was worth a regiment of KGB. I was above even Berea in Stalin's eyes. No one could touch me. Everyone feared me. If they saw me eye to eye and lived, they breathed a sigh of relief," Alex paused, drawing a long breath.

The young man was engrossed in this story of power. "People with that kind of privilege did not usually last long in Stalin's regime in the thirties, the Red Army Purges showed that. How did you escape?"

"Easy. I left Russia at the first possible chance. That was when he decided to back the Loyalist Government, and we formed the International Brigades."

"Stalin let you go? Didn't he want you to carry out the dirty work of killing Generals in Purge?"

"He called me in," said Alex. "He said the Trotskyites had to be eliminated and the best way he knew was to appeal to them and to join together in the International Brigades to defeat Franco. They came in and formed the PUON. As soon as they did that, Stalin said that those were my targets. I was to go to Spain as the bodyguard of Walter and begin the systematic elimination of all PUOM officers and men who distinguished themselves in combat. We'd give a PUOM officer a medal at noon, feed him a great lunch, and then I'd come in during the siesta and shoot him.

"It was really very simple. Stalin loved it and told me to stay until the end. He was mulling over sending me to Mexico to kill Trotsky but some yahoo volunteered to stick a pick-ax in his head in Mexico. It was just as well, I might have had to shoot Frida Kahlo and I liked her work," Alex said, a slight smile forming on his wrinkled face.

"And Stalin, when he died..."

"We killed him, too, Kruschev and the lot. Stalin was getting crazy. He was anxious to start another big war. He did not seem to understand that the United States possessed the means to obliterate every city in Russia. He had to go, so," Alex shrugged, "he went."

"You mean you ..." the young man got no further with his question as Alex interrupted.

"What does it matter who? It was all of us. It doesn't make any difference who pulled the trigger." Alex snapped his fingers. A silence fell on the room as the young man digested the momentous piece of history. The, the assassin shook himself out of his reverie. He was here to kill Alex. What did it matter who pulled the trigger? Alex was an embarrassment to the present regime. He could not be allowed to live.

Recognizing that the tome had come, Alex stood up slowly and went to the liquor cabinet. He pulled put a very old, dusty bottle of vodka.

"You know what this is?" he laughed. "Of course you don't know. How could you? This bottle of vodka came from the private stock of the Emperor, Czar Nicholas. My father was in the execution party the night they killed the entire family. Before he died, the Czar asked for his own private bottle of vodka – the very best in the world. My father brought it to him, gave him a drink and took a drink himself, then shot the Czar. He kept the bottle and passed it on to me. 'When you shoot a great man, take a drink," my father told me. 'You'll have this bottle a very long time.'

"He was right of course. I shot hundreds of ordinary men, but a few great men. I drank a toast to Lenin, Stalin and Trotsky. Berea, maybe, I can't remember."

The interrogator stood up, put his arm in his overcoat pocket. Alex heard the click of the safety and held up his hand.

"Hold on, young man. Call the policeman from outside."

"Why? I don't need him."

"To witness it," Alex said matter-of-factly. "There are going to be people who will forever question whether you actually killed me. People create legends from phantasms."

"Quite right," he said, opened the door and blew his whistle. The policeman came trotting up and entered the tiny dacha one more.

"Now gentlemen, since I am facing the wrong end of a gun for the first time in 80 years, permit me to orchestrate my exit," Alex said. "I've no reason to try and escape, I've nowhere to go and I'm damned tired of this boring life."

He set up three shot glasses and poured the Czar's vodka. The interrogator signaled to the policeman that he would explain the importance of the vodka after the deed was done.

Alex opened a cabinet and produces two large, dark brown Havana cigars. He lit the cigars for the men.

"I'd join you, but the doctor says they are bad for my health." All three men laughed loudly at this. Alex then opened a drawer and produced two boxes full of H. Uptmann's and gave each man a box.

"A souvenir of my time in Havana," he said graciously.

"You were there to eliminate Fidel?" The KGB agent asked.

"No, Che Guevera. Fidel is still alive."

"Oh, of course. Lenin, Stalin, Berea and now Che." There was no reply.

"Okay. One last favor and we come to the final curtain." He wheeled out a sort of bench with drawers in both sides. Atop it was a huge Victoria. He pulled out an old 78-rpm from a tattered paper sleeve. "Ah, the piece d' resistance."

Alex blew on the record as it to remove the dust from its surface, tested the player's needle on his finger and wound up the ancient Victoria until it was wound tight.

"In Spain in 1938, a young man from New York came in with the Abraham Lincoln Brigade. He was a Captain, and that rare thing – a millionaire Communist. I liked him immediately, and after dinner he played me this record. It was a huge hit in the United States. It was a Cole Porter song, 'Begin the Beguine,' and it was recorded by a brilliant clarinetist named Artie Shaw. You've heard of him?" Alex asked.

The young men both shook their heads side to side.

"Ah, so. Just as well. He was tall, very handsome and had a prosperity for marrying beautiful women. You've heard of Lana Turner, Ava Gardner?"

Again, the two men shook their heads.

"Of course. Prehistoric times. Still, the music caught me, and I was taken so I shot the officer and kept the record. It survived the Spanish Civil War, the Great War and many lesser conflicts. So gentlemen, I'd like you to hear it and, right in the middle, when Artie Shaw hits a high not, I want you to carry out your mission. And, by the way, the young American Captain was PUOM, so ..."Alex pauses a moment, then continued.

"I was one clean shot at mid-forebrow. In this way my face will be untouched and recognizable in photographs so that your word can never be challenged. You have the policeman as an eyewitness and a photograph of a dead 80-year-old assassin. You think you can do it?" he looked directly in the eyes of the young agent.

"Of course. It's very kind of you. Do you think we could hear the song through one time, so we know exactly when the high note comes?" he asked.

"Excellent idea!" Alex rubbed his hands and beamed. "That way I can hear it all the way through for the last time myself. Enchanting. Great touch!" the old man said, delighted.

He played the record, keeping time with the yellow pencil he held; at times dancing nimbly to the beautiful music, and stopping to note the exact time he was to be shot. Then, the record stopped.

"One last thing, I promise," Alex said. "This needle is driving me crazy. It's used up and scratching the record. Do you mind terribly if I change the needle so at least I go out listening to the pure beauty of Artie Shaw's clarinet?"

"Of course," the young man said and loaded a bullet into his gun chamber.

Alex went around the back on the bench where small drawers held equipment to maintain the old Victoria. Without hesitation, Alex drew a Luger from the drawer and, before either man registered what was happening, they were toppled over on their backs, a neat hole in their foreheads.

Alex replaced the needle and played Artie Shaw's "Begin the Beguine" all the way through.

"Amazing," he thought. "Mr. Shaw got one successful hit from this song, and I've gotten hundreds of hits from it."

Now for 60 years I had been avoiding disturbing Artie Shaw, and then, suddenly, in a few days my wife wakes me from my nap and says, "Artie Shaw is on the phone."

Once, a famous writer friend of mine, who was also Artie Shaw's pal, found out about my Artie Shaw fixation and he warned me. "You like Artie Shaw? You like his music? Good, never meet Artie Shaw. Never. If you are at a party where he is, run like hell in the other direction." Why? "Because he will not let you talk. He will dominate the conversation so that it's all about him."

"Yep, I read 'The Trouble with Cinderella.' I know of his self-involvement."

His book, "The Trouble with Cinderella" was done in the early fifties after Shaw had left music forever. It was a piece of self-analysis after years and years of psychoanalysis. It was one of those: Who am I? What does this mean?" books that middle-aged millionaires write after they succeed in business and fail in life. There was very little about the music business. The book dogged me.

I read it and left it on a plane before I had finished it. I found myself in the Air Force in basic training in San Antonio's Lackland AFB in mid-summer. I was made a corporal because of 8 years of college and all my degrees. I marched the flight to K.P. and looked for a place to hide. Found a base library, decided to re-read Artie Shaw's "The Trouble with Cinderella." Where to hide? It was hot as hell. Under the library building looked cool. I crawled under there, read the book, fell asleep and was rousted by two nonliterary MPs. An ignominious end. I never finished the book.

My next sighting was worse. A few years ago we were in Baton Rouge to do a Showtime fight on a Saturday in summer. Hot as hell. Town deserted. I am bored; spot a library across the street. I walked over on a whim, looked up, you got it, Artie Shaw's "The Trouble with Cinderella." I pick it up and I am reading through it pretty good when a bell sounds, library closes at 6:00 p.m. I still haven't finished the damn thing. What to do?

I'll just take the book to my hotel, read it through to the end, and then, Boy Scout that I am, return it to the book return slot. I walked comfortably out and the entire place goes bananas. Burglar alarm! Condition Red! A book is being sequestered by terrorist. The Taliban are making a movie on Artie Shaw's "Trouble with Cinderella."

Acute embarrassment as I am taken before a stern hatchet faced old Daughter of the Confederacy. Christ, they are worse than nuns.

I apologize profusely, offer to buy the book. Rent the book. Do anything she wants. Donate money to the Building Fund. Anything, just don't call the press!

"No," she says with finality. "The book stays here!"

"But I only want to read the last hundred pages."

"Come back Monday, when we open again," she says, her lips pursed, a hard look in her Confederate eyes.

To tell the truth, I was so scared that she would recognize me and call the papers. I can see it.

Fight Doctor Caught in Burglary in Baton Rouge.

Tried to steal Artie Shaw's "The Trouble with Cinderella."

It would make the wires. God. The shame of it.

"Stealing an Artie Shaw book? Artie Shaw? Not Aristotle, not Shakespeare, not Byron, Shelley or Keats? You mean, Artie Shaw writes?

Isn't he the guy that married Lana Turner and Ava Gardner? Did he play "Begin the Beguine" and "Frenesi"? I thought he married his eighth wife and died. He is dead, isn't he? Or, am I thinking of Guy Lombardo?

Once safely on the street, I swore to rid myself of the Artie Shaw curse.

But, as you can see, I can't get rid of Artie Shaw. And I am now talking on the phone to Artie Shaw himself.

"Why is he following me? Can you tell me, please" I moan into my pillow.

Sample Shaw sightings at random:

1. I buy a wonderful WWII tape "The Story of G.I. Joe." It's a story of Ernie Pyle. Robert Mitchum in his first starring role. Burgess Meredith. The company is in camp first night in North Africa. It's World War II.

Background music: someone is playing Artie Shaw's "Summit Ridge Drive." Shaw did not sue for patriotic reasons. He was in the Pacific without a long distance telephone.

2. Great Spanish art house movies called Recuerdos (memories) in Spain. This one's a long, long shot. A boy and a girl fall hopelessly in love during the siege of Madrid. They have to part. He takes "their song," a record, with him into combat.

They lose track. War is over. Each marries another. 40 years go by.

The man returns to Madrid from America, a widower, to return the record now scratched and cracked to his former lover. She is also a widow. They meet: they play the record. They sigh. They cry. Christ, they are both 70. The record: Artie Shaw's "Begin the Beguine." Shaw does not sue.

3. A comic book movie Rockateer with luscious Jennifer Connally and Alan Arkin. She is gorgeous, and is being courted in a 30's Hollywood nightclub with a big band playing. People are dancing.

Who? Artie Shaw and his band. The entire band, in white tuxedos with a guy who looks just like Artie Shaw is playing (what else?) "Begin the Beguine." (Shaw is suing.)

4. A T.V. movie on the Life of Judy Garland. She is 17 and has a huge crush on Artie Shaw. He is 30, plus a few wives. Discourages her. She tries suicide. Mercifully, no "Begin the Beguine." (No lawsuit, also, no Shaw music, and a big Shaw disclaimer.)

5. I do a great comic oil painting of Artie Shaw as a 60 year-old out of shape man in his BVD's and undershirt, playing to an old fat tarty Lana Turner. It is pure comedy. I sell for it $5,000. To Crazy Joe, one of Tampa's legendary characters.

Crazy Joe shoots Artie Shaw in his velvet slippers, right through the A, with his French automatic. (No lawsuit from Shaw.)

New York Times Sunday Entertainment Section headlines:
Artie Shaw, 91 issues new CD.

Artie Shaw? 91? Hell, I thought we were both dead.

## Hearing From Shaw—The First Time

Since my stroke a year ago, an afternoon nap becomes an obligatory event. I don't have a choice. If I am not asleep by 3 PM all systems in my body automatically switch off. I'm not good for anything, and I collapse in bed for a restorative two hours of sleep. I have no choice.

The news that Artie Shaw, himself, was on the phone turned on all the dormant systems.

"Artie Shaw? Yes, I'll talk to him."

Shaw got on, his voice had a slight pleasant laugh in it, and it seemed very familiar to me.

"Ferdie, how the hell did you dream up this fantastic short story? It's funny as hell."

Any conversation which opens with "Ferdie" not Doc or Dr. Pacheco is a roaring good start. Shaw sounded like he knew me. Like I was an old friend. What the hell? Our conversation took off on that note, like two friends who had not spoken for a long time and were getting back together. Shaw was bright, funny, self-obsessed, opinionated, very aware of life around him, and kind in his remarks. After a long spell, which was a Shaw monologue, because he is now hard of hearing and a phone conversation is difficult, Shaw wound up our pleasant time. He abruptly invited me to visit him at his home in Ventura, California. My heart jumped. Boy, would I like to do *that*. To ask all those unanswered questions that Henry and I fretted about? God, yes, but I was under travel restrictions by my neurologist.

"I'd really love to do that Artie, but my stroke doctor forbids me to take a plane."

"Take a train," said Artie, always ready with an answer.

"Look, Artie, my mother-in-law lives in Denver and she is 82, and not feeling well. I may *have* to come to Denver. If so, I'll hop over and see you."

"Great, try and do that," he sounded sincere. Maybe his curiosity was aroused. What makes an intelligent, successful, creative person follow a foolish obsession such as my collecting Artie Shaw Sightings over 63 years? What is it he wants? It was to be one of his first questions to me. He needed to know.

"What the hell is it you *want*? What can you *get* out of me? This is the thing that has puzzled me all my life," Shaw said.

"What is it the public wants, expects, out of the Shaw thing? The public should only be interested in my music. Not me. Not Artie Shaw the person. How can knowing about my personal life enrich anyone? I'm just a guy that got lucky early in life, and stumbled along after that, tripping, falling, picking myself up, and I just kept on keeping on. The business of Artie Shaw is what I still don't get. You tell me. Why did you come across the country just to talk to me?"

A good question, to which, I had no answer. As in most things that great afternoon I found I agreed with Shaw a lot. Restraining myself from thrusting an 8x10 glossy of Shaw in 1939 to ask for an autograph, with a lame: 'I guess a quick autograph is out of the question?' I said simply, "I don't know." Since I became almost famous myself because I stood next to Muhammad Ali all of his fights, and then did 25 years of Network sports casting, which included TV exposure for all the important fights, specials, heavyweight Championship fights and three Olympics, I had a taste of people who want to know all about me. Why? I agree with Shaw. What is it they want? The business of Artie Shaw was the price he paid for the music of Artie Shaw. Fame and fortune had a stiff price for a thinking man like Artie Shaw. Like Garbo, Shaw just "vanted to be alone." I could dig that.

## Getting Started for the Interview

As in any attempt to have a 73-year old man meet a 93-year old hermit, a glitch developed almost immediately.

Artie Shaw depends on his man Friday, and any time you get a third man in a transaction, things start to go wrong. Shaw had suggested coming over on a Sunday when his secretary was there and could fetch things for us. Shaw was not as mobile as he liked.

Sunday came with a medical disaster. My mother-in-law took a turn for the worse. I had to rush her to the hospital to put out the fire. Luisita, who handles everything in my life, phoned Shaw's secretary to make alternate plans. If things went well at the hospital, I'd take a plane to LAX on Monday, take a motel room, get my rest, and see

21

Shaw Tuesday for lunch. The secretary was to make a reservation at the motel in Ventura. I took that as a solid agreed upon plan.

When I was safely ensconced in my motel room on Monday night, I called Shaw to tell him I'd arrived and would be at his house, ten blocks away, at 12, lunch, as agreed.

Shaw was blustery and sharp and very negative. "I can't see you now. You said Sunday. I waited all day Sunday. You can't just keep me waiting until Tuesday! I won't see you."

Clearly the secretary had dropped the ball. The secretary was off on a 2 week vacation. Artie Shaw was alone in his house. He couldn't get to the front gate of his fortress to open it.

Trying to conceal my disappointment and rage, I began to smooth-talk Shaw out of his high dudgeon and into working out a way to open his front gate. He has a fifty-ish Irish housekeeper whom he called his baby sitter, who was off that day, but who might come if he could get her.

Sounded better. I was still steaming. "Artie, I didn't come across the country to meet you after 63 years of tracking you to get shut out by your secretary's miscue. I'm going to see you today if I have to scale the wall."

Shaw laughed, "Don't worry, I'll fix it."

When he called, in about 10 minutes, Luisita had her camera case packed, the tape recorder batteries checked, and 1 sketch pad in hand; we were ready to go. Then another Shaw thunderclap.

"Don't bring *anything* but yourself."

"My wife," I began.

"No wife. No PR guy. No camera. No tape recording. This is just a social afternoon between two guys."

My wife Luisita is an expert professional photographer. She has been by my side all my big moments. Her photos of Ali are collector's item. I need her camera; I need her working the tape. I need her producing and editing skills. I need her opinion.

Shaw was adamant. It wasn't worth blowing the meeting so I went to have my meeting with Shaw. I wasn't sure how shitty he would be. It was a bad start. It didn't look good.

The old gatekeeper was very cheerful. She greeted me, "You must be an old friend of Mr. Shaw's, he's all happy and bright this morning."

Emboldened a bit by that, I walked to a large parlor. It was packed with books, records and many photographs. On a large couch sat Artie Shaw like a sultan. He seemed in good spirits, and very relaxed.

"Ferdie, you look much lighter in person than on TV," he said with an apologetic laugh. "TV puts 10 pounds on you."

'Aha!' I thought. 'Gotcha!' Shaw knows me. He has watched me for years on TV—he loves boxing and Ali—and, oh boy, I'm in. It's a trade off. I'll tell him my Ali stories; he'll tell me his Artie Shaw and the Big Band stories. This was more like it. Now, I thought, what would Henry like to know from Artie Shaw?

I bearded the lion in his den, and what a den it was. Shaw does not live in splendor, he lives in comfort, surrounded by the trophies of a rich and full life. Books and records overflowed his bookcases and lined the walls. Photographs filled the tabletops and any available wall space. Artie Shaw had lived a full successful life and he looked like the King of the Manor as he sat on a big sofa propped up by pillows, looking dapper, cool and collected. An oddity struck me. There was nothing about Artie Shaw that suggested a ninety-plus old man. He simply didn't *look* like an old man.

Artie Shaw was generally conceded to be the best looking man to lead a band. Charlie Barnet was handsome, and matched Artie in that he had eight wives, but aside from that, Barnet was not in Shaw's class in looks or music.

I expected the famous face to be caved in by the erosion of the years. What a shock to face a man who is still vital and still physically handsome. His face had aged sure, but in the best way. He was still striking as a man. He has his share of illnesses, but none is as debilitating as his inability to hear. Shaw is a conversationalist. He likes the give and take of a stimulating conversation. People say he talks too much about himself. Well, pardon me, but did I come across the United States to talk about me, or am I here to satisfy all the questions Henry and I wondered about. Hell yes, Shaw talks about Shaw, his music, his clarinet, his wives, his views on life. I knew about *my* life, I wanted to learn about Artie Shaw. Shaw got right to the meat of the matter.

"Ferdie, I don't understand. What is it you want from me? What can I give you? Why do people who like my music always want to meet and know me? What is it I'm supposed to do for them?"

"In my case, I am a historian. I set out to document my time on earth. I wrote many autobiographical pieces, and you remained a sort of ongoing mystery. Henry and I listened intently to every record you made. Henry would try to copy you note for note. He almost blew his brains out doing "Concerto for Clarinet." That was some solo."

He laughed. "That was a misnomer. It wasn't a concerto. Lot of that piece was scraps from one place or another."

"The opening was stuff from 'The Blues.' "

Shaw smiled. "You really do listen. This piece was ordered by Hollywood. We were making *Second Chorus* and they said, 'Artie, do something like "Sing Sing Sing" by Goodman.' I hated that. Copying is not my style. But the structure was the same and we ended up with a tom-tom ride out. But, you know what, for years that is the way I ended all my sets."

"Wasn't that hard as hell to do? That is a lot of clarinet."

"I never thought of it as tough. I'm a clarinet player whether on the first number or the last; clarinet playing is what I do.

"Do musicians tire of a number? Yes, although I always approached it as the playing of music is what we do. If one tune is popular, you close your brain down and play the damn thing. It took me years to get used to the idea that fans want you to play your solo exactly as you did on the record. I thought you had to keep exploring to find a freshness to bring to the piece through changing the jazz solo. Eventually I gave up and played the record."

"Didn't the musicians rebel?"

"Hell yes. One of the best piano men I ever had was Dodo Marmarosa. One night he comes to me and says, 'Artie, if we have to play 'Frenesi' more than one time tonight, I'm gone. You'll never hear from me again.' And that night, sure enough, the late arrivers who have missed 'Frenesi' kept bugging us to play it again. I did, and when I look over to the piano, Dodo had split. I never saw him again.

Author's Note: As I write this on 9.26.02, Dodo Marmorosa has passed away. A mysterious man, Dodo had a strange beginning. As a teenager he palled around with Buddy de Franco. They got into a fight with a gang of sailors who beat the boys up badly. They held Dodo over a railroad and pounded his head on the rails until he went into a coma. It took him a long time to recover. From then, for the rest of his life, he was not quite right, and was considered a character. Shaw considered him one of the best piano players who played with his band.

"Once I was talking to Goodman and he told me a story that kind of threw some light on the subject. Benny practiced six hours every afternoon whether he was playing that night or not. He never missed his six hours of practicing. His wife, a very educated and cultured lady finally could not stand it and asked him, 'How can you play six hours of scales and the same songs you've been playing for years and years?' Benny thought about it for a moment, put the clarinet down and said, 'You know while I practice I notice you are out in the hot sun six hours day after day. The weeds grow back; you go back to work. You do the same thing day after day in the hot sun. I've often wondered, how can she do that.'"

Shaw laughed at the mention of Benny, his perennial rival. No one I know can come to a clear definition of who was better. Henry eventually gravitated to Benny; I stuck to Shaw.

I heard a certain softness, a caressing and respect for the melody in Artie Shaw. His tone was soft, easy to listen to, melodic, lyrical. No one else played like Artie Shaw and plenty tried.

Goodman was a phenomenal technician, and he swung. His physical appearance was that of a Jewish CPA, or an absent-minded professor. Whenever Goodman appeared he out swung any musician in the house, white or black. Musicians gave up trying to cut Benny. Benny was a Jazz Phenom. There was Louis, then there was Benny. Once, Ellington had written a particularly hard solo for Barney

Bigard, and the clarinetist played it under severe protest until one day Duke, ever the master motivator, took aside Bigard and said, "You know I sent your solo to Benny to play and see if it was do-able. Benny sent your solo back with a note: 'Barney Bigard is the only clarinetist who can play this right. *I can't*, it's too tough for me.' Barney never complained again.

Shaw laughed. He seemed to like any mention of Goodman.

"Once, in London, after I'd left the music business for the second time, I saw Benny in his hotel. There was Benny, three hours before the concert, still going over 'Poor Butterfly,' 'One the Alamo,' 'Limehouse Blues' and all the repertoire. 'Benny, for God's sake, you've been playing that shit since 1936, don't you think you know it by now?'

"'Artie, it's part of the job. It's the only way I can keep up the level of excellence I demand of myself and my musicians.'"

Clearly, Shaw did not agree.

"Well, then, who was the better clarinetist, you or Goodman? I decided to straight for the jugular.

He grew pensive. "Hell, who knows the answer to that: We were totally different. At one of our meetings we talked about why he heard his clarinet different from mine."

"I don't understand all this bullshit about playing behind a note—to lay back; to caress the note. Hell, man you see a B flat on the chart and you hit a B flat perfectly on my clarinet. That's it, that's all there is to it. "

"There is a difference, Benny, 'I said to him.' You play the *note* on your clarinet; you play the clarinet. I play the *music*. That is where we differ."

I had never heard it explained better. If I'd heard that I wouldn't have wasted hours arguing the point in our vast ignorance with Henry. Looking back, we were just like everyone else in the music world. No one could figure who was the best. Both were great instrumentalists, take your choice after that. It's still the same today.

I heard Henry in my head, 'Ask him about the reeds. Did they make a difference?'

Shaw made a face. "Reeds, plastic or bamboo. Different, but in the end, you adjust, and it does *not* affect your playing. Man, in the Pacific during the war, that was our biggest problem, keeping the freshness, and plastic or not, reeds were our biggest problem."

"That and I read your instruments disintegrated in the heat and humidity of the South Pacific."

"My poor clarinet was held together with airplane glue, rubber bands, paper clips, and it was a major effort to get a sound out of them. Any sound.

"I always prided myself with keeping my bands perfectly tuned. I insisted on strict musicianship. In the Pacific all that went out the window."

"I'd heard a strange comment from you about Duke Ellington's 1941 Band. I feel like Duke had his best band of all time in 1941, much like BG and Artie Shaw. 1941 was a bumper year for jazz bands, cars, and movies. What a year for excellence. Well, what about Duke?"

"Best bunch of musicians in any band. They were all stars. How could you beat Johnny Hodges, my choice for the best alto man in the world, and Henry Carney, the rock solid baritone sax. Sonny Green on drums. Lawrence Brown's velvety trombone, and an entire all star trumpet section.

As good as they were, that band was *always* out of tune. They worked so hard, played so many gigs they didn't have *time* to tune their instruments. Duke knew it but just shrugged. Too busy working to tune up. "A band out of tune was unforgivable to me at the time."

Most people I talked to over the years widely admired Shaw as a musician. He could write a hit song, write the lyrics, do a great big band instrumental chart, and was without peer in having the best ear in music. And he knew how to criticize and teach. He knew, he sensed, what every man in his band was playing. He had great ears.

Artie reports seeing Les Robinson not so long ago and he thanked Artie profusely. "Thanks for being so patient. You stuck with me for a year while I tried to get the sound you wanted out of my horn. Finally, one night, I got it. I got the Shaw sound. He was happier than

I. He's won. He had faith that I was a good musician, and he knew the Shaw sound was hard to achieve."

The other day I ran into a beautiful ex-jazz pianist, who had a great record. Her name was Nancy Reed. She was good enough to play in the BG quintet, and sing, and compose songs.

She and I have done long jazz hours on radio, so she was delighted to hear I was finally talking to Artie Shaw. This is how she saw it now, 40 years later.

"Artie was so much more musical and was (and still is) so fresh, and he is still the best musician among all of them. In any era."

Why is Shaw so different? Why can't anyone copy Shaw?

"As a doctor, you know every man is anatomically different, different lips, teeth, tongue, pharynx. We all have our unique sound.

"In addition to that, I began to 'hear' in my brain what I wanted my clarinet to sound like. But, try as I might I couldn't hit it 100%--the best I could do was 95%. I wanted my bands to sound like the sound I heard in my head. They rehearsed and rehearsed, and we came close on a lot of records. We were different."

Buddy Rich, who kicked the Shaw band so hard he lost his job said to me, "Shaw is the brainiest guy in the band business, and the best musician. He knew *exactly* what he wanted the Artie Shaw band to sound like. I had a ball with him, the band was so fine, and Shaw utterly astonishing. He fired me. I was too loud. I wasn't playing in the Buddy Rich band. He took me to Dorsey, and said, here's your star. Tommy turned me loose."

For proof, dig out the commercial recording of *Carioca*. Then go to the location gig recorded at the Blue Room of the Hotel Lincoln in New York City. Wow! What a difference a great fresh 18 year-old drummer makes!

"Buddy was just a kid. 18 or 19. He'd been pestering me to play. That night, Cliff Leeman was sick, I said, step in, and the roof fell in. We just couldn't stop. In that set we played *Rancho Grande*, disregard the hokey vocal by Tony Pastor, and listen to the ride out. That is another sample of a band on fire, and the leader leading the pack. I just felt we were flying and if you want an example of how

Buddy was bigger than the band, pick out the *Traffic Jam*, our main killer diller. He blows us off the stand. He hadn't learned to be *part* of the band yet. He did better with Dorsey and he loved to play with James. By then, he's matured. I think he reached his pinnacle with his own bands which seemed to reflect his abrasive, in your face music. Rich was great."

Rich responded, "Later in the Harry James band I put all that knowledge to good use and I became a big band drummer."

Shaw laughed at the mention of Rich. "A huge talent, but what a bad boy! Between him and George Auld they were always fighting and keeping the band in turmoil. And Buddy was a dynamo who equated playing the drums LOUD was the same as GOOD.

"Much later, after he was a solo star for Dorsey, he formed his own band, and then, he learned to fit in. Those bands played hard and were excellent musical aggregates due, I think, to what Buddy learned from me and Tommy Dorsey, and Harry James. But he was a pain in the ass."

That he was. But he was evenly matched with Tommy who was pretty contentious himself. Can you imagine what it must have been like in that band with Tommy, Buddy Rich and a young Sinatra? There was a fight every night. Once Sinatra hired some mob guy to work over Rich, who ended up in a hospital. After that they became buddies.

"How do you rank Tommy Dorsey?" I asked.

"As a bandleader, he was great. He kept that brawling band together. We started together and he was as good as any trombonist on the scene, and he had a very sweet, very cool sound on his horn in the ballads. Then, the booze and the years stripped him of his abilities, and some nights he couldn't make the high notes in 'Marie' and the band would laugh at him. That was sad. He outlived his talent."

"Is that why, at 34 you quit the clarinet flat? Put it down and never went back? Were you afraid of going out like Dorsey, unable to play at the top of your form?"

"That was undeniable some of it. But at 34, I'd reached my goal. I *did* get to 100% with the last Gramercy 5, and so I could go no higher.

"People don't know it but I went out on a concert tour playing only classical music. I played Mozart, Ravel and all the classical clarinet pieces. I just wanted to see if I could do it. Naturally I got no publicity. People who are interested in 'Frenesi,' are not drawn to Mozart. It is a different discipline. You *must* play Mozart, there is no room for Shaw. When I got through, I'd proved it all to my satisfaction. From the top of the mountain the other side is downhill. No thanks, I wasn't looking forward to the downhill ride. I decided to quit flat.

"Another thing, Ferdie, I was tired of the music business. Everything about it bothered me. I was especially hacked at the record executives. What their qualifications were for the job, I could not guess, but they had the job *not* because of their knowledge of music, nor for intelligence, which made no sense. Let me illustrate.

"My Gramercy 5 was created to compete with Benny's Quintet and sextet. I wanted a different sound. I came up with a harpsichord. The public ate it up. We scored big with our first sides, 'Cross Your Heart' and 'Summit Ridge Drive.' The sides were different and they swung nicely for listening and dancing.

"We made several more successes and suddenly I was called in to talk to one of the suits. 'No more Gramercy 5', the suit said brusquely.

"Why? They are selling briskly."

"Our board feels that the public is *sore* that they are paying 50¢ to just hear *five* musicians. For half a buck they deserve the full band."

"Stunned and amazed I had to conform to my contract and we made no more Gramercy 5 sides! How do you live with that shit? I didn't. I *couldn't.*

"One day I woke up overwhelmed. Did I need the stupidity of the music business? No. Could I live without being a part of it? Hell, yes. Could I live without playing the clarinet? I thought I could. As it turned out, I did. Put it down never picked it up? I was right. It wasn't indispensable to my life."

"You virtually gave up your *identity.*"

"Yep. Kinda. Hell, I *was* Artie Shaw, and I was in the Artie Shaw business. There were a lot of things I wanted to try, and I seemed stuck in the music business."

"Like the milk business? A dairy?"

"I agree it seems wacky now. But I wanted distance from turmoil, publicity, the music business. The agony of my frantic existence. I wanted quiet."

"Still, the dairy business?" I shook my head. The dapper, sophisticated Shaw in overalls?

"I made money," he said in a mocking self-deprecating way, in a kind of defensive way.

At that moment, I heard an inner voice say, 'What are you kidding *him* about. Didn't you get out of all medicine at 50, without anywhere to land? What is crazier, give up the clarinet or give up medicine? Medicine was *my* identity since childhood. I loved being a doctor. I began a feel a certain kinship with Shaw. He wasn't eccentric or crazy—he had his reasons and they were valid for *him*, you, the public didn't matter. He did what was good for him at the time. So did I. I could dig it.

I heard Henry's voice in my head, 'Ask him about swinging the classics.'

"My favorite of your 'swinging the classics' was 'Softly as in a Morning's Sunrise,' and the 'Indian Love Call,' and 'Rosalie' from 'Rosalie.' Whose idea was that?"

"Well, I liked the music of the Operettas, they had some great composers, and I was young and frisky, and felt they deserved to be played. No one else in the band biz did, so we had a kind of a monopoly on Operetta. I still like 'em."

There are moments a fan etches in his memory. I can remember the exact circumstances of our bringing home two Victor record by a new band you put together in L.A. With strings, violas, violins, it was supposed to be lush music.

31

We were not prepared for the lush sound of "April in Paris," "Dancing in the Dark," and "Moonglow." Henry's big phonograph reproduced the sound, a shock wave of appreciation shot through my mind. I felt like I was falling through a velvety, cushioned tunnel, so deep, so soothing. It's time like these I felt I wanted to get up and dance like Fred Astaire, light as a feather with Ginger Rogers in your arms. It was so soft, so romantic so *right*. So beautiful.

Out of that period came two of the most popular Shaw sides of all time. After his Mexican exile came "Frenesi." On that recording date they had some of the best musicians in the country, Skitch Henderson played piano. But the jewel in the crown was "Stardust" with Billy Butterfield. Shaw loved his open trumpet sound, and musicianship. Shaw turned him loose on the opening solo. It was a stunner. Than the soft band played with feeling to what some consider one of Shaw's best solos. I think it's the best solo anyone ever played on "Stardust." I have Benny playing "Stardust." There isn't a doubt who captured "Stardust" best.

The other night I sat with Ballet Master Edward Villela at the restaurant Palms' opening, and he invited me to the premier of his new modern music suite to be done in four sections. I was shocked when he said:

"You'll love the last jazz piece. We are dancing to Artie Shaw's 'Stardust.' It's going to be a gas."

"Why 'Stardust'?"

"It's the finest piece of the war era. It is a perfect piece of music."

"Well, as I said to Henry, if *this* is the new band, I'm not going to miss the old band." We played the sides night and day. The pleasure that music gave us! It formed the foundation of our memory of that era.

Eventually, Shaw, I felt got more and more brainy and he left the visceral feel of jazz behind. In time, even I had to admit it was not swinging at all, but was elevator music with the superior Shaw clarinet to save the day.

Why "Evensong"? "Suite #8," "The Maid with the Flaxen Hair"? And even the incomparable "Summertime" by Eddie Sauter?

"That was listening music," said Shaw. "I wanted to play up to the potential of that band, with arrangers like Eddie Sauter, how could you not record such quality music? You didn't dance, you sat back and appreciated it."

"Is it true that you wrote 'Any Old Time' for Lady Day to record with the band?"

"And wrote the words. I thought Billie Holiday was the greatest woman singer I ever heard. But she had inner demons which made it virtually impossible for her to function inside a big band family. She had a short temper, much shorter when she drank or was high which was virtually 100% of the time. She was quick to take offense, particularly any remark she took to be a racist slur."

"You had to record that again?" I asked.

"Again; suits and then senseless judgment calls. Our record was going great with Billie. The suits yanked it and made me record it with Helen Forrest. I loved Helen but she was no Billie. I felt ashamed that we had to do that to Billie, but we did it anyway."

"Helen Forrest was the best pure band singer of our era, she worked with Benny, with me, and ultimately with Harry James. She was no Billie, but she was the next best thing to Billie, minus the hang-ups."

What a soap opera her involvement with James produced. If you were looking to write a tragic love scene no one would do better than what happened to her with James.

Harry James seduced every band singer who ever sang with his band. He was a great ladies man. Tall, handsome, and with a great personality, every woman fell for him. He was easy to love.

But none fell harder than Helen Forrest who was a nice sensible middleclass Jewish girl from New York. Benny and Shaw had hits with her vocals. She was the best pure band singer around.

As they all did, she fell hard for Harry. The romance was kindled by several million sellers during the war. James and Helen Forrest were linked together. James having gone bust with a hot jazz band, found the money cow in funding soft-hearted romantic pieces designed for the lads overseas and their lasses who stayed home pining for them to return. "I Don't Want To Walk Without You,"

"You Made Me Love You," a syrupy sweet "Sleepy Lagoon," and "It's Been A Long, Long Time."

Shaw grunted, "Harry made his pact with the devil. He gave up his place in the Jazz Hall of Fame. He gave up jazz and adopted a sweet style. He made millions, married a movie star, and then ended up broke, discredited and without his family. Harry James was a tragedy."

Shaw commented on James, who paralleled Shaw because both were prodigies on their respective horns. Shaw sought that elusive 100% perfection, James took the cash and the easy way. Faust won. James lost.

"Are you familiar with the German artist George Grosz?" asked the erudite Shaw.

"Indeed. As a cartoonist he was one of my big influences. I didn't care for his art once he got safely ensconced in a teaching job in America. He seems to have lost his fire." I could see where Shaw was going. This was a parallel with Harry James.

"Once at an art exhibit of his work, an old crusty New York Art Critic came up to George, and in front of all his friends she said in an angry voice, 'Mr. Grosz, as long as you were in Germany, in danger for your life, drawing those wonderful Goya-like acid etchings of the sins of the Weimar Republic, you were the best artist in the world.

'But once you came to America, you shed the acid pen, and started to paint the beautiful bucolic America with a broad palette. They're beautiful, but they are *not* art. To me they look like pretty postcards. In short, Mr. Grosz, you have sold your soul to the devil.'

'Madame, I have been waiting 25 years to sell my soul to the devil and *he hasn't made me an offer yet!*'"

Shaw laughed. I laughed. Perhaps George Grosz did not sell his soul to the devil, but Harry James did.

Shaw seemed lost in thought about the waste of a huge jazz talent like Harry James. "Ferdie, did you ever hear the set of records he made with Teddy Wilson when they were both with Benny? If you want to hear what a great trumpet player James was, listen again to those sides. James was a great instrumentalist, first, last and always."

"Back to our soap opera," I said determined to run this by Shaw.

They had come to the part of the romance where James usually fled. But Helen heard James had bought an engagement ring. They were scheduled to sing on a huge V-Disc Overseas Xmas broadcast, and scheduled to sing "You Made Me Love You." As the highlight of the show it was their big signature hit record.

She bought a new dress, and sat prettily in front of the band expectantly. Harry was introduced to a loud ovation. He raised his arms for silence. "Boys, I'm here to give you G.I.'s over there a big surprise."

Helen got ready to get up. The big moment, the ring, the best selling #1 love song in America!

"Boys, tonight, for the first time you're going to hear from the next Mrs. Harry James..."

Helen gets half up.

"Betty Grable! Yes, the #1 pin-up of the U.S. Armed Forces had agreed to marry yours truly."

Out strides the stunning Betty Grable, kisses James who places the ring on her finger. The band strikes up and they both perform "You Made Me Love You."

Helen Forrest sat back down.

And later it took a squad of New York's finest to pull her off the ledge of her hotel.

Shaw smiled a knowing smile. "Betty was a wonderful girl, and I'll tell you right here, Grable had the best body of all, including Lana, Ava and the lot."

Shaw ought to know, I figure. A Shaw sighting popped into my head. I couldn't resist. We were headed for forbidden territory where Shaw could terminate our meeting if he felt insulted and his privacy invaded.

"Phil Silvers tells a story where you three were walking down the street when Shaw stopped at an expensive jewelry store. 'Look at that watch,' he pointed to a lady's watch. Betty Grable's heart started to beat. Shaw did not bestow expensive baubles to his babes. She gushed; they went in.

'Put it on; see what it looks like,' said Shaw. Betty placed it on her delicate white wrist. It looked great!

"What do you think Phil?" asked Shaw.

"It's great, Artie. Great."

"Good. I'll take it, and can you change the band to a *man's* band?" Shaw tells the jeweler. *No wonder* she ended up marrying Harry James.

Shaw waved that away as if it were a pesky fly. "Where do people get those stories?"

"It wasn't true?" I pushed.

"Well, kinda," he said with a mischievous smile. "I wasn't the nicest guy in the world when it came to gifts.

"Once I got carried away and bought Betty a sapphire and diamond anklet. She was so thrilled she would take it off. She went out on stage, and danced with it on. When she came back it was gone.

"Boy, was that a panic. The stagehands closed the curtain, turned on all the lights and began a foot by foot search. They found it, and Betty was spared an embarrassment."

Shaw laughed good-naturedly. "Maybe. There are so many of those stories around even I don't remember what is true or not."

Given this opening I plowed on into forbidden territory, the Shaw voyage into matrimonial turmoil. I took a deep breath. Where to start? At the beginning, of course.

You just went out to Hollywood to make a little movie called *Dancing Coed.* It was a studio potboiler used to introduce their new sex kitten, 18-year old Lana Turner. Everyone expected fireworks, but they fussed and fought instead.

"We were both suffering from the same disease, Self-love and self-delusion. I was too busy loving myself to have time for her. So was she. We avoided each other. Then one night the phone rang in my apartment and it was Lana. She was miffed. Her fiancée, man-about-town Greg Bautzer had called to cancel a dinner date because of work at the office. She was dressed with no where to go. Would I take her to dinner?

"Forgetting our difficulties on the set, and remembering very well what a stunning girls she was, I impulsively said, 'Be right over.'

"The night was golden. Lana looked as great as an 18-year old can look and she was fun, flirtatious and kept daring me to do one thing after another. Finally we got to an airport. We rented a plane. We flew to Arizona. 'What is there to do in Arizona?' I asked. 'Get married. People fly to Arizona to get married,' said the luscious Lana Turner.

"So we did."

I have had a lifetime to think about this. Where was my brain? My maturity?

"Wait a minute," I hold up my hand. "You were supposed to be the most level-headed, intelligent musician in the world. Some even dared speculate that you were an intellectual. How could you possibly consider marrying an 18-year old starlet?"

Shaw was nodding his head, smiling as if he had heard the question 100 times. "Wait a minute. You have *your* view of that Artie Shaw. Let me give you what it actually was.

"I was about 26. I was famous and rich. But for six months all I had done in Hollywood was work hard as hell with my band. We rehearsed, played dates, rehearsed again. All the time I was fixated on my band. To the exclusion of *anything* else. By that I mean female company. I just had not had the time to bother. God knows, in Hollywood of that era, there was certainly a surfeit of available lovelies. I could pick and choose, but I chose my music over the girls.

"Then one night, at 26, rich and famous gets an invitation I could not refuse. When I got a good look at Lana Turner, in full battle gear, walking toward me, I lost my head. Love at first sight? Hell, yes. And much more *lust* at first sight. At that point I would have married her mother if it meant bedding the 18-year old angel. Then, on top of that, she was so much fun. I followed her with my tongue hanging out, dare after dare until, I woke up in Arizona. 'What the hell do you do in Arizona at midnight?'

'Get married,' said Lana flashing her million dollar smile.

"I'm telling you Ferdie, the intellect is not connected to the pelvis. No contest. You get married, and so, we did."

What happened to that blissful arrangement?

"When the pelvic action abated somewhat I found that while Lana Turner was an industrial strength sex animal, the rest of the time she was an empty flower pot. She was shallow and vain as only an 18-year old #1 starlet at MGM could be."

"I launched on a program of education. Unfortunately, Lana was not into education. She was perfectly happy to be shallow, vain and the number one starlet on the MGM lot.

"Eventually, in mid semester, she got pregnant. We were both kinda happy. Me more than her, I think. Then one weekend I left to play a weekend date out of town. When I got back on Monday Lana was not pregnant any longer. What the hell? Mister Mayer of MGM had ordered an abortion and America's number one starlet agreed. Without even telling me." Shaw kind of sat up. "And *that* was the end of *that* marriage. I didn't feel I had to explain myself; I just split."

"Of course it's easy to leave Lana Turner if you have Ava Gardner walking up ahead on the highway of matrimony." I reasoned, although Shaw didn't marry Ava until after the war. "You never carried a torch for Lana?" I said using the jargon of that time.

"To forget a beauty, get another one. I can't really compare the two, but Ava had an animal-like quality, like a jungle animal, and a stunning face and figure. And, what Ava wanted, Ava got, and little Ava wanted me. Did you know I named our Gramercy 5 hit 'The Grabtown Grapple' for Ava's hometown?

"Ava was just as beautiful, but she was funny and brainy. It's just she was a guy as far as morality. What she saw she went after. I was victim number two. She used to say what she needed was a down-to-earth regular blue-collar Joe. Yeah, I'd say, like Mickey Rooney, Artie Shaw, Mitchum, Lancaster, Dominguin and a whole quadrilla of bullfighters, Gable and Kirk Douglas, and the most unhappy ill-fated coupling with Frank Sinatra. All plain as dirt blue-collar workers. We remained close friends until she died."

"She enrolled in the Shaw school for Undeserving and Unthinking Young Starlets, and actually did well for six months. Ava was very bright, and she had a sparkling wit. We wandered apart as is often the case where there are two stars in one house. And Hollywood toughened up this sweet country girl. She got ruthless. She got tough.

Many years later when Ava wrote about her marriage to Shaw she said, "Still and all, Artie was one of the deep hurts of my life. I was so much in love with him, and I don't think he ever really understood the damage he did by putting me down all the time."

And, "Of my three husbands (Rooney, Shaw and Sinatra) I had the most admiration for Artie. He's impossible to live with, sometimes even to be friends with, but he is a worthy human being and an extraordinary man."

The above quotes were taken from her autobiography *Ava*, written at the end of her life. They maintained close friends her entire life.

I remembered a night in Miami when I found myself out with Debbie Reynolds. The sweet little Tammy had grown tough as a cob. Her observation, "Show me a female star who has been on top six years, and I'll show you a guy."

Shaw's ability to jettison himself out of a bad marriage caught the public fancy. Shaw tells the story of a pal stuck in a hideous marriage for 20 years.

"How did you do it? How did you walk out?" the unhappy man asked.

"As soon as you are sure it's not going to work, you march into your closet, get the biggest bag you can carry, and load it up. Get in your car and check into a hotel."

"That's all there is to it?"

"Yep, that's all."

"Yes, said the stricken man, "but what do I do for a piece of ass *tonight*."

Shaw threw his hands up. Once on the Carson Show he was introduced as the nation's leading expert on marriage. Shaw interrupted, "No. I'm the nation's ;leading expert on *Divorce!*"

Perhaps an unusual view of Shaw in matrimony came in a Shaw sighting from ex-wife Evelyn Keyes book.

Evelyn Keyes had had rocky experience on the matrimonial ship, having suffered through abusive marriages to John Huston and Michael Todd. To taper off a duet of beating she boarded the Artie Shaw Intellectual Ship of Matrimony. She found that physical and mental beatings were, in fact, the same.

They went to live in Spain. Shaw bought a castle on top of a mountain. The price was cheap, $400. The townspeople laughed at the American millionaire. They had stuck him with a castle on top of a mountain, which had no running water.

Undaunted, Shaw, figuring that there *must* have been a natural supply of water when they *built* the castle, hired a hydraulic engineer, who drilled down and discovered a pure crystal clear water spring. Suddenly Shaw had water, and enough left over to go into the water-selling business. Leave it to Shaw to out think his enemies.

Shaw retired to write. Evelyn Keyes describes the morning.

Shaw would count out and stack his white sheets of paper. He would sharpen his No. 2 Eagle pencils, all the same size, and he would sit for hours to produce maybe two sheets of story. Every morning.

The end came more dramatically when they were visited by a prominent Hollywood couple and decided to go into town to have lunch. Things were going along great, when they decided to go into a café for lunch. Shaw excused himself to go to the bathroom.

Shaw emerged enraged. He had discovered that the last button on his shirt was missing. Since that button is below the waistline, no one could see it. Shaw could. He screamed at Evelyn in front of the astonished Hollywood couple. "Look, I take care of your every need. I feed you, I clothe you, furnish a castle for your shelter, and all I *expect* from you, is that you take care of *my* needs."

"But it is only one button. I'll put it on at the house," said the shocked wife.

"You don't have a button, you don't have a needle and thread? What the hell good are you?"

End of the Spanish idyll, end of the castle in Spain, end of Scarlet O'Hara's sister. Pack your bags, grab an airliner back to the U.S.A. You are toast, sister.

Artie smiled sheepishly while I told that story waving his hand wearily, "Yeah, more or less something like that happened but, as usual, there's much more. She was a ball-busting competitor. She'd been with John Huston and Mike Todd. She was used to fighting for everything. Everything was a contest, so it blew up. So what?"

Artie Shaw married eight time. That's a lot of repetitive mistakes. I asked his view of matrimony and he came up with a jewel of a Shawism.

"Marriage is the end of a perfect affair."

"If I could have just stopped myself when the affair was hot, and listened to Cole Porter's words, 'It's too hot not to cool down.' I would have had a tranquil romantic life."

I was getting nervous, because I don't think any man wants to dwell on his mistakes, much less *eight* mistakes. I decided to summarize and split.

"Of all your wives, which were the worst?"

"That is easy. It's a draw. I decided enough of the dumb actresses, I'd marry an intellect, so I picked Kathleen Windsor, who had written a best-seller, *Forever Amber.* She was a mano a mano daily screaming match. She was deadly."

Artie stretched out on the couch, shook his head, as if to wipe out any memory of Kathleen Windsor, then as an afterthought he said, "Of all the women I ever knew she was the most unmitigated bitch of a cunt I knew."

I thought it was time to move on to Doris Dowling , the mother of his son, Stephen.

"I got another non-actress in Doris Dowling, a multimillionaire ding bat. I think she beat me in the number of time we got married.

"The brilliant, witty director Billy Wilder had also been a Dowling victim. Along with several other alumni we met in a Beverly Hills lounge. Comparing notes, it remained for the sophisticated Billy Wilder to sum up what we all felt. 'She is summed up in one beautiful, incontrovertible word, She is a *cunt.'*

"With the other three at least I got beauty and a lot of beautiful moments. With these two, unremitting hell." Shaw shook his head, remembering an awful moment. "At one point, Doris Dowling pointed a revolver at my face, and *pulled* the *trigger.* Luckily the gun's safety was on, and she knew nothing about guns.

"Next morning, over an argumentative breakfast I asked, 'Last night you pointed a gun at me and pulled the trigger. Did you mean to kill me?'

'Hell, yes,' she snarled, 'I was mad as hell at you. I wanted you dead.'"

End of that story. Doris Dowling had a son with Artie, but much as Artie wanted to be part of his life, she kept them apart for most of the boy's life. Now, in later life, Stephen and Artie have a nice warm relationship, but thanks to Dowling's bitchiness they were separated all of Stephen's life.

Now, *that* is *my* definition of a cunt.

The talk of ex-wives was beginning to oppress me and I could see Shaw was not very happy reliving old battles.

I decided to switch moods, and since Shaw had shown a decidedly good sense of humor I thought I'd go down that trail.

"Artie, you must have had your share of zany players. Can you think of any great stunts they pulled?"

Shaw sat quiet for a minute, smiling. "Not right off the bat, but later I wrote a whole funny book called *The Best of Intentions* and that'll give you some stories."

I decided to kick start him with the funniest story I ever heard concerning a bandsman.

Woody Herman came into New York with his First Herd and scored a resounding success. After a great Saturday night concert they were all invited to a swank party in Long Island. It was lavish and well attended by swells and celebrities.

Woody had a fat bass player, before Chubby Jackson, who found he desperately needed to go to the bathroom, but they were all filled. The hostess magnanimously offered her bathroom upstairs, and admonished him to be careful around the bed, since the guests had piled their furs on the bed.

The fat man cold not find the light. In his desperation, feeling around the room for a light switch, he had knocked over a bottle of what he assumed was perfume. Finally, he found the light, relieved himself and came back into the bedroom to find that had knocked over a big bottle of jet black ink! It was all over the white rug, and had even splattered over a few white fox furs. Embarrassed, and scared to death, he rushed out and took a cab back to New York.

The next day, when Woody called this lady, she was the soul of gentility, forgiving the error, not asking for a cent, and was generally wonderful.

Woody called the bassist in and told him he was off the hook due to the kindness of the hostess, and that he must return to the mansion, bearing a large bouquet of flowers and apologize in person.

Greatly relieved that he was off an expensive hook, he splurged on flowers and went out to see her. The butler told him to wait in the library, the hostess would be down in a nonce. The butler takes the flowers up to her.

Once again the bassist finds himself in a darkened room. The butler says to sit in one of the big leather chairs, and leaves. While it is not the black blackness of the bedroom, it is a penumbral gloom.

He heads for a dimly perceived chair and plumps himself heavily into the chair.

"Yip!" he hears a strangled sound. He jumps out of the chair. He looks down; he has sat, and crushed a tiny Chihuahua. No doubt about it, it is dead.

In a panic he picks up the crushed body and, finding no where else, he puts the little dead dog in the piano, and closing the lid of the piano, he leaves.

The story ends there. Woody never found out and the band was long gone by the time anyone found the carcass.

Shaw laughed at that, and, as I knew he would he came back with his story.

They were having a party on a rooftop in New York. It was the top floor of a nine-story building. It was more a literary soiree than a normal cocktail party.

Shaw, and many guests, were annoyed by a yapping, yipping small dog who was running around biting ankles and generally making himself annoying. Truman Capote, in particular could not stand the dog.

The owner refused to lock the dog in the apartment, started to play catch-the-ball in an effort to quiet him down. That diversion proved louder and more disruptive than anything.

Finally, the ball came to rest in front of Truman Capote, who promptly kicked it *over* the railing, the dog in hot pursuit. Those on the ground floor said they saw a dog, with a ball in his mouth, sailing serenely into the concrete.

Shaw laughed at the story. So did I.

"One final story. About the craziest of the jazz men, Joe Venuti.

"Oh man, *he* was crazy. If he'd have been in my band I would have killed him. One day in Washington, DC, when he was in the Paul Whiteman band, they were appearing in a large sold-out amphitheater. The star of the show was Roy Rogers and his horse Trigger.

"Joe was seated at the end of the violin section, his chair almost in the wings. Bored, he looks to the side and sees Trigger right next to his chair. With his bow he begins to stroke Trigger's very large member. Soon, it gets to be very, very large like a harpoon.

"When Roy Rogers takes the stage center and pulls his horse up on two legs to greet the audience, the sell-out crowd gasps, and breaks out into loud gales of laughter, leaving Roy stunned and perplexed."

Shaw is laughing again, He has a nice pleasant controlled laugh. The kind comics at the Friar's Club have, where instead of laughing out of control, they make reserved laughing sounds and say, "Now, *that* is funny. Funnnn-ay!"

I asked Artie, "How much could you take?"

"One day, as my contract was running out, they called me and *ordered* me to change an ending to a piece I had just scored myself. It was a different ending and fit the piece. I flat out refused. I walked out of a Victor contract and into a Decca. Not that the "suits" were much different there."

You know Artie, that story, the creative artist versus the executives exists in all layers of creative work. Consider the dolts that hold those jobs in the movies, TV executives, sports executives,

Broadway producers, book publishers. It's not something that's unusual.

"That's true. Only I didn't have to take it because I had "fuck you" money. My records sold. 'Begin the Beguine' (4 million), 'Frenesi' (3 million), 'Stardust' (2 million) and 'Dancing in the Dark' (1 million). Don't you think that should have shown the "suits" I knew what I was doing? But, since I had "fuck you" money, I just walked when they got too stupid."

O.K., let's go to your famous vanishing act in 1938-9. You were making $26,000 a *week*, an astounding sum of money for those Depression times. "Begin the Beguine" was a big hit, as were other numbers in the band. You had topped BG as the King of Swing in the polls, most critics claimed you were the King of the Clarinet. You'd been married to two of the most beautiful women in the world, Lana Turner and Ava Gardner, and, yet, without warning you vanished. Why?

"I was a confused and agitated young man. I didn't understand the demands of celebrity hood, I was a musician, hell bent on getting my music played right, getting my clarinet to sound the way I heard it in my head, and with little desire to be a "star". I couldn't understand why people chased me down the street to pull buttons off my coat. I couldn't understand why kids paid for a ticket to hear the band, and then stood in front of it and yelled at the top of their voices for the whole night. Hell, most nights I couldn't even hear myself *or* the band. Why? That's why I called all jitterbugs morons. I felt I was sliding into a complete breakdown, physical and nervous. I had to get away to save myself. I picked cold turkey. Just walked. In retrospect I was right. I came back from Mexico, bigger than ever, and completed my Victor contract with four sides, all huge winners with over a million sales each. They were 'Frenesi,' 'Stardust,' 'Dancing in the Dark' and 'Moonglow' (I think)."

But 'Frenesi' came back and bit you on the ass.

(Shaw laughs ruefully.) "Yeah. I was lying on the beach in Mexico listening to the fishermen chant as they worked their nets. The song I heard was 'Frenesi'. I loved it. I went back to my room and wrote an arrangement. Then I went home. The band I formed was large, it had strings, and a lush, soft sound. It fit *Frenesi* perfectly. We sold 3 million bucks. In 1940 that was huge. It remained a big hit through the war years. And then, one morning, a little Mexican gentleman with a briefcase showed up. It was *not* an original fisherman's work song. It was the work of a Mexican composer Diego somebody, and had already been recorded by Xavier Cugat! That cost me a million or so."

I was in college then. Our biggest "make-out" slow dancing song was 'Stardust.'

"I cut that because I had recruited Billy Butterfield into that band, and I loved his big open horn. He had a perfect, full sound. So I just turned him loose on the beginning solo. I also feel it was one of Jack Jenny's best trombone solos. Jenny was a vastly under rated trombone player. If you follow my discography you'll see how many times I featured him. And, of course, I had been playing 'Stardust' for years, and I loved it as pure solo material. Yes, I thought that was as close to perfect as you can get for dance music."

Might I include "Moonglow" in my personal list of make-out pieces.

"I went into the Navy immediately after that and was amazed at how many records had been sold of that one recording session. Also the Gramercy 5 sides *Cross Your Heart* and *Summit Ridge Drive*, seem to have the beat for swing dancers. The nickels flew into record machines."

Let's talk World War II. You don't ever talk about your Navy experience.

"The absolute *nadir* of my life. I've been trying to block those years out.

"When the war started I found myself playing *Stardust* one night before a college audience, and I felt that it was so meaningless to play these dates when the Japs were kicking our butts so bad. Miller had gotten a good deal from the Air Force, so I thought I'd try the Navy. Again, my naïve self saw an easy transition into a Navy band. After all, I was as big as Miller, and I was a star soloist. Glenn was just a band leader. And, by the way, the Navy had turned down Miller, and he ended up an officer in the Air Force.

"Not only was I not given a commission, but I was given *no rank* at all. I served as a regular gob on a minesweeper. It was very tough duty, physically exhausting, and dull as hell. The first time I hit dry land I put on civvies."

Wasn't that a jail offense in wartime?

"Yes, straight to jail. But hell, that wasn't all. I went AWOL, took my car and drove directly to Washington to the Pentagon. I meant to see Forrestal, the Secretary of the Navy."

Boy, you don't fool around. You're going to the top guy, no chain of command for you, out of uniform and AWOL into the bargain.

"I was so desperate to get off that minesweeper that I would have preferred the Brig."

How did you get on?

"The Artie Shaw Thing got me as far as an admiral who had never heard of *Begin the Beguine* or Artie Shaw.

"I assured him Forrestal was a personal friend. I got through on the office intercom and he came right out and hugged me. The admiral's jaw dropped.

"I pitched my idea for an All-Navy jazz band, I'd head it and donate my entire band-book. I just wanted the Navy to maximize my value, and to bring the best I could to the servicemen of the Pacific Fleet. I didn't want to play for Officer's Clubs in the rear areas. I wanted to play for front line troops.

"Just like that he made me a Chief Petty Officer, not an officer rank like Glenn Miller got, but still the highest non-commissioned rank available. I got carte-blanche to recruit my band. I went out and got the best damned jazz musicians I could get. What a great band that was!"

I'm sorry they didn't record it. Miller got wide publicity and push from his Air Force band. Why not you?

"Ferdie, there were no recording studios in the South Pacific. We were in a war down there. We were shelled from the sea, bombed from the air, snipers in the trees shot at us. Man, that band deserved combat pay. Records? Hell, I just wanted us to get home in one piece."

You had one of my favorite drummers in that band. Davie Tough.

"Ah, one of my favorite drummers. Light touch and a master of the brushes. I went out and scraped him out of a gutter and dragged him to a Navy recruiting post. As you know, Davie had a bad drinking problem, he was then to the point of anorexia, bulimic, and about 100 pounds soaking wet.

"The Navy doctor looked at me: "This is a joke, right Chief? This guy doesn't need to be in the Navy, he needs to be in a hospital!" I laughed, and explained how great a drummer he was, and how I needed him to complete the band I was forming.

"The doctor made him do a few graduated squats, each a little deeper. By the time Davie got to a full knee bend he passed out, face down on the floor.

"The doctor and I picked him up, revived him, and swore him in to the U.S. Navy. As much of a physical wreck as he was, he never missed a date in the Pacific.

"I loved Davie Tough. Too bad he let the sauce beat him."

After about 2 years in combat the entire band fell apart.

"It was a complete and total disintegration. Our instruments fell apart in that heat and humidity. My clarinet was held together with rubber bands, glue, Band-Aids, and Scotch tape. I could barely get a decent sound out of it. I personally had every type of fever that you would get, plus amoebic dysentery and every type of fungus and parasite around. The worst of all was the Malaria. Man, that was tough to take.

"The band came into port and all of us checked into the hospital. We were exhausted, depleted, demoralized, and finished as a band. We never played together again. And, Ferdie, it was a *great* band. We had the top caliber musicians. For example on piano we had Claude Thornhill, a pal of mine. Who was also a great arranger.

"I just wish I could have recorded a few sides."

But your reception wherever you went must have been unusual.

"One day we were flown out to do a concert on a big carrier in 1943. The war wasn't going well for us. Each naval engagement brought fearful casualties. Carriers in particular were choice target of the crack Japanese aviators.

"I had no way to anticipate that this day I would experience an epiphany, a sort of bright shining moment which defines your life.

"We landed on the deck, and it was swarming with sailors, and they were yelling non-stop. The elevator started to go down. The next deck had hundreds of sailors yelling. The next deck, the same thing. The final deck had all the officers of the carrier, and *they* were yelling at the top of their voices. The cumulative effect of this shaft of loud sound was so great that we could not start to play. It went on for almost half an hour. No one could stop it, as no one *wanted* to stop it.

"Finally it occurred to me. I've reached my moment. I'm not just a musician, I'm not just a clarinetist trying to be the best, I'm not just the band leader of the number one band in the country. What I am is part of the culture, of the home front, of America. To these guys *Begin the Beguine*, brings all sorts of memories home. To hear the Artie Shaw band was to suspend the reality of the South Pacific war, and to be back in the States in the arms of a beautiful girl. I had reached a higher plane. Quite simply, I had become part of Americana.

Author's Note: At this point my painter's mind clicked on. I determined that I would paint a six foot tall painting of Shaw in the well of that carrier with hundreds of Gobs hanging onto every structure. I did it and sent it to Shaw entitled "Shaw's Epiphany."

With as low a rank as you had, and as strong-minded an individualist as you are, how did you handle the brass?

"Badly. Once an officious rear admiral ordered my band into New Guinea. Well, the fighting there was at its worst. There were nothing but jungles and Japs. I told him, "I'll be damned if I am going to expose my band to that danger." He barked and threatened me. He *ordered* me. I said, "I'll go, but you can't order me to play. I'll take my band, but *not* my music. My music belongs to me by law. The Navy has no jurisdiction on my music." That was that. I won. Not to say that I didn't lose a few, but, by and large, by the end, we understood each other. We weren't just a bunch of jazz musicians out on a lark. We were combat vets; we'd been bombed, shelled, strafed and exposed to sniper fire. We demanded, and got, respect from the other combat vets.

"All in all, it was an experience I'd like to forget. It was awful. I don't think my body and mind ever recovered.

"When I went into the Naval Hospital I was a total wreck. I actually wanted to die. I couldn't do anything but lie in bed, a burned out hulk of a man.

"Beside a collection of tropical diseases, I had malaria and amoebic dysentery. Worse than all the physical illnesses, I was an emotional wreck. I didn't know who I was. I did not want to get out of bed. Each day was an agony or despair. I felt I would never be able to function again as a musician, and, I found, to my surprise, I didn't care. Hell, I didn't care if I lived or not.

"As soon as the doctors won the battle for the health of Artie Shaw, they began to schedule me for psychotherapy. I did not resist, I welcomed it.

"If there was a point in my life where bad things turned into good it was my year of psychotherapy. I found, to my great surprise, about myself. My real self, not the Artie Shaw Thing. Me, the real me. Well, who in the hell was that? I had been so busy proving myself, getting to be the best clarinetist around, getting to be a big cheese in a Big Band Pond, that I had neglected myself.

"But, who exactly was Artie Shaw, the person? I peeled away the layers of my psyche, a piece at a time. I worked out a lot of hidden hostility, answered some disturbing questions, and slowly began to feel better about myself. It took a year but it saved me. I've been a devoted follower of psychotherapy."

It was curious to me that in reading Ava Gardner's book *Ava*, she should evaluate Shaw, thusly:

"Dear Artie, Wherever you are I wish you well, and thanks for the memories and guidance. And I'll make you a little wager, I'll bet you are still in analysis up to your eyebrows."

Shaw winced slightly. It's true he came to depend on, rely on analysis. It helped him get through the day, and Lord knows, with the hassles *eight* wives put him through he *needed* some outside help.

Shaw sniffed on his pillows. "Analysis is good for some people, others didn't need it. I needed it, period."

"Finally I was well enough to try to return to my life as a musician. I had not played the clarinet for over a year. Tentatively, I picked it up, and found, I was rusty, but had not forgotten how.

"I needed to 'work out' and that beautiful band leader, Count Basie offered his band. I loved that band. The musicians were all first rate, the arrangements were solid. I did radio shows and found that all of my power returned unaffected. After a few dates I shook hands with the guys of the Basie Band, and shoved off, back into the world of music. Was I happy? Not very, but, as usual I needed the money."

We got up to get something from the upstairs bedroom and work area.

The staircase told the Shaw Story. Each step was stacked with books. His bedroom looked like an old book warehouse. It looked like my house.

The walls were covered with old 8x10 glossies of the various bands, awards, old friends and assorted bric-a-brac. I kept thinking about the moving problems incurred in eight divorces. He must have kept the Seven Santini Brothers busy.

There was one thing missing. No music paraphernalia. No music stand, no sheets of music, and no clarinets. You'd be hard pressed to guess you were in the bedroom of the premier jazz clarinetist in the world. It was as if he had set out to irradiate all traces of his old life.

So, I decided that was the place we would attack the subject of the clarinet and his place in the history of the instrument.

"Let's talk clarinet, Artie, do you acknowledge that you are the best of all clarinetists?"

Artie's eyes crinkled good naturedly, "Me and Benny. But the *style* differs with each man who tries to dominate the instrument. It's really *not fair* to compare."

"Why?" I asked.

"I 'heard' my horn in my head. I heard the notes, one tone or so behind the written note. I heard a softer, smoother, warmer note. At first it eluded me. I almost got it when I played alto sax in studio bands, but then I switched to clarinet, and the notes began to approximate what I heard. I knew I had gotten the style I wanted, the Artie Shaw style. Why doesn't someone copy it? Because they are not physically built like me, because they don't hear what I hear in my head, because, perhaps, they are not willing to pay the awful price of practicing hour after hour. Who knows? I know I got mine, go get yours."

Does the instrument make a difference? Reeds?

"Every instrument is different. I've had a few. Pre-war French Selmers are great. The wood from which the Selmers are made came from a forest in France. In WWII a whole flight of B-17's dumped their bomb loads on the forest obliterating it. It'll be 100 years before they can make these French Selmers again."

As to reeds. Always a problem. I don't see any difference between bamboo or plastic. Each has its own advantages and disadvantages.

I asked, what got you to play jazz? Was there one guy who drove you to play?

Shaw responded immediately, "Yes. There is only one influence in jazz for all jazz men. It starts and stops with Louis Armstrong. In the early thirties I drove from New York to Chicago just to hear Louie. I arrived early and sat right on the lip of the stage. When Louie came in he played a startling solo on *West End Blues* to introduce a piece. It blew me away. The beauty of his line of thought, the clarity of each note, the sheer musicianship made me dream of a time when I could blow like that.

Why did you change from top alto sax studio musician to clarinet, and why not both?

"I found a home, a comfort zone with the clarinet. I did not think I would be taken seriously, if I played both. One or the other, I thought, and *I* correctly picked out the clarinet."

You finally finished the Shaw voyage in jazz in 1954. Didn't you think you could continue to play, and play progressively modern jazz? Others who did, and did so with big bands, included Woody

Herman, Stan Kenton, Les Brown, Count Basie and Duke Ellington as well as Benny Goodman.

"I was just tired. Played out. Tired of the hassle. With the "suits", the club owners, the fans. The whole thing was not interesting, and I had no economic need."

But here it is in 2002, and you are still a name, still interesting enough to deserve page 1 of the Sunday *New York Times* Entertainment section. No one has heard you play a note since 1954. Why do they still care? Does it bug you that you are still in the Artie Shaw Business?

"That's because of the recordings. They were good then; they are good now. Do I mind? Hell, no, as long as they don't find my house and attack me. I still get letters. They want my photo and autograph. Why? I could never understand that at all."

Did you ever have a favorite band? One that met your rigid standards?

Shaw laughs, "Yeah, in 1949, I found myself in a bind with Internal Revenue, and I had to form another band to pay them off. I got together a collection of superlative contemporary musicians. A great voice in that band was pianist Dodo Marmarosa who was fresh from working with Bird, Diz and the Bop movement. Herbie Steward, alto man, one of the Four Brothers with Woody's band, a hell of a section leader. We had a tight trumpet section with Don Fagerquist, and two tenor stars in Al Cohn and Zoot Sims, and my old reliable Irv Kluger at drums."

I remember some good sides, but no big "hit". What happened to the best band?

"A flop. No one wanted it. I think it was just too good, too musical for its time. After all we had a new book by composer arrangers like Gerry Mulligan, Ralph Burns, Mary Lou Williams as well as the old stuff by Eddie Sauter, Ray Conniff, Buster Harding, and Jerry Gray. Man, I looked forward to playing with that crew every night."

So what became of that band?

"We recorded some tunes which were not promoted and haphazardly released.

"I still owed the IRS, so I formed a rinky-dink band, got stock arrangements, and went out to do dance dates until I was free of debt. On my last night the owner of the dance hall shook my hand and told me what a pleasure it was to have heard the band, what good business we did, and finished with, "This is the best band we've had in here since Blue Barron!

"That's it. I quit. Once and for all."

Which brings me to the subject of the 1954 Gramercy 5 six-week gig at The Embers in New York. Now, while this is an interview of you, I'd like to give you a rest, and give you a view from outside Artie Shaw. Is it true? Let's see.

Tal Farlow, the great guitarist, is my source. We spent a night discussing this date. Let me read you my interview with Tal Farlow and get your reaction.

Tal Farlow told me Artie got together a Gramercy 5 to play The Embers in New York. These were the top professional progressive musicians in the land. The crème d l'crème. Hank Jones, piano. Joe Puma, guitar. Tommy Potter, bass. Irv Kluger, drums. On the record session I did in New York in March 1954, we also had Joe Roland, vibes.

Artie got us together with the promise that he wanted to push the music, to play what he heard, to have no boundaries, no limits. He wouldn't dare ask us to recreate *Summit Ridge Drive* or *Begin the Beguine*, in the old, popular accepted way. This would all be fresh. Instead of the standard swing rhythm section, we would use a Bop drummer and, so on. He agreed, but he said he would only pay scale. Now, all of us were getting top dollar as recording artists. Scale was an insult, but, all of us admired Shaw's musicianship so much, and the opportunity to work with Shaw when he was opening himself to experimentation with the new music, was worth the cut in pay.

We rehearsed for a few weeks, and Shaw was astonishing. His musical knowledge was vast, all encompassing. At certain points he passed Bird, or Diz, or Miles in his creativity. I'd never heard *anyone* including Artie Shaw himself play the clarinet like that before. I thought we were about to make jazz history, the second coming of Artie Shaw. It was thrilling.

Shaw, smiling for the first time since I started to quote Farlow's version of that gig said, "This is the point where I finally hit this 100% of the music I heard in my head. It was exactly what I'd been trying for since I picked up the clarinet. Didn't you *hear* it?"

Artie, I'm not a musician. I heard you sounded different, softer, more mellow, not as hard piercing as with your jazz band, but I was not as sophisticated a listener as a professional musician. I'll confess that as a dyed in the wool Shaw fanatic, it *sounded* different, not necessarily better. What did you do differently to get that sound?

"Well, I had been playing a lot of Mozart, and works like Ravel, Debussy, and Shostakovich. That caused me to approach the clarinet differently. The vibrato which made me sound different in my popular work, changed to a ripple, rather than a wave.

"I even changed clarinets, from a Selmer to a Buffet, which has a warmer more woody sound. I place my clarinet *next* to the mike rather than blow into the mike. This produces a very light sound. Sometimes one can even detect the breath sounds or hear the clicking of the keys.

"This was my 100% sound and hard as hell to do. I was keeping the volume down where I used just enough breath to keep the reed vibrating. In fact, any less air and the sound would just stop.

"If you listen to *Yesterdays* or *Don't Take Your Love From Me*, you'll hear that I was on the verge of not being heard. The sound I had been wanting, looking for, all these years was just that, a warm highly emotional sound, that I don't think can be done much better. And that answers my question, why haven't there been imitators who can capture the Artie Shaw sound on clarinet.

"And that's why I put the clarinet down and never picked it up again. I'd gotten to 100%, reached my goal, and as I said before, saw my death before me. In fact, that was so hard I don't know if *I* could have maintained that level of play as I got older. I didn't want to go back to the 97, 96, 95%. I'd had it. I'd climbed Mt. Everest."

Back to Farlow. At the end of say six weeks Artie was satisfied, the musicians were happy as hell, and they opened at The Embers. And, then—disaster.

The curtain opened, we started our set amidst big applause, but, No Artie Shaw! There was a buzz in the crowd as we finished the whole set and Artie had

not showed his face. I rushed to his dressing room where Artie sat fuming. Shaw said, "Did you see that audience? 90% women. They're not in the room to hear our new Gramercy 5, they're here for the 'Artie Shaw business.' They want to see what I look like, move, act, talk, anything *BUT* hear how I play. They will hear me, but they want *Begin the Beguine* and *Frenesi*."

So I said, "Fuck em, we're playing your old hits, but we're playing them *OUR* way, with the new jazz sound, and you are playing like you've never played before. Go out and kick ass!"

Eventually, with the owner of the club yelling, Shaw came out and, sure as hell, we couldn't *hear* ourselves play because of the yelling, just as Artie had feared; what's the point of playing our wonderful book, if all we heard was drunken broads yelling at the top of their lungs. Artie was right. Jitterbugs, even middle-aged ones, all *morons*. I felt bad as hell for Artie. Oh Lord, six more weeks of this.

Doggedly we played our stuff. Eventually people came in who wanted to hear the "new" Artie. The critics and the New York musician crowd dug our stuff. It *was* great music. But the majority of the crowds were not as satisfied. They wanted the *old Summit Ridge Drive* and Shaw's resolve started to crumble.

Midway through, Shaw fired the Bop drummer and hired his old swing drummer, and slowly we slid back to the old *Summit Ridge Drive*, and we young hard-headed progressive musicians resented the hell out of that, for we had agreed to take scale, if Shaw would promise to play progressive stuff. Slowly, set by set, Shaw sounded like he was milking the audience for applause, seeking approval and courting adulation. Shaw denied it and we ended the engagement with relief.

I asked Tal, "You mean there were hard feelings?"

"You don't know Artie. He has no feelings. He is a block of ice. On the last night we were offered another six week extension. We huddled backstage and agreed that we would play the six weeks *at scale, if* we could go back to our progressive jazz, but if he continued his retrogression to swing, we would go on, *BUT* at our normal high fees. I was delegated to take that back to Shaw."

And it went over like a lead balloon?

Farlow described the scene: Shaw was drinking a cup of coffee and reading the newspaper. I knocked, entered, and said my piece to the back of his head. I said that was our price or we would quit. Without pausing a beat, or turning around, Shaw said, simply, "Good bye."

Now, after six weeks of playing together, *that* is a cold fish.

What good sides do you recommend from that session?

*I've Got a Crush on You, I Can't get Started, Summit Ridge Drive, Stardust.* All of the sides we recorded in March 1954 in New York hold up pretty well.

I don't think I ever heard a clarinet played better. I don't think anyone will ever hit that perfection that Shaw got from his instrument. That alone made the gig worthwhile.

Artie made a face and shrugged. Well, yes and no. Everyone experiences and sees things differently. It was a nice point to step out of the music business. I left. No regrets.

Do you miss anything from the first half of your life? The music? The bands? The public figure part of it? Your place in the history of Jazz and American Popular Music?

"I missed the ability to do anything I want. You are the boss, absolute, when you lead a band. I miss being the Captain of my ship."

At some point did you have an awareness of what you had become in America, the measure of your fame, your impact on America?

"Yes, I think mine came on that carrier in the Pacific. The roar we heard was inhuman. Their joy on seeing us, hearing us in person, was a high I never experienced again. That night I thought to myself, "Damn Artie, you've created a good chunk of Americana; something lasting, and I can't think of a better legacy than that."

In the hey-day of swing 1938-45 who did you regard as having the best bands of that era?

"I think the four bands that best represented that era, the giants, if you will, were Benny Goodman, Tommy Dorsey, Duke Ellington and me.

There were many good bands right under that big four level: Gene Krupa, Harry James, Les Brown, Claude Thornhill, Count Basie, Woody Herman, Stan Kenton and such.

Many of those bands stayed in business for decades, many are represented today by "clone" bands, including the Artie Shaw band. What's your take on those imitation bands?

"They play the same book as the original band, and they add "new" arrangements and contemporary tunes. Of course, they are not the same. Who can play like Benny, or James, or Gene Krupa?"

Or you?

"Well, the kid Dick Johnson plays my solos pretty close, but he plays his own solos on the new pieces his way."

Could you have spent your life in front of a band in which you have ever-changing sounds with the new younger and younger musicians, as Woody Herman did? Or Duke Ellington and Count Basie?

"I didn't. Enough said."

Didn't you miss *music*? What did you fill your time with?

"Things which interested me. Writing mainly filled my days. I produced movies, had a successful dairy farm, became an expert at rifle target shooting. Whatever interested me I went after. I was never idle, never bored. Life has never been dull."

Talking about producing a movie, which you did very successfully with *Séance*. I heard *Second Chorus* was a horror to go through. Why?

"I'd written a treatment of a book I liked about a kid who was a great jazz trumpet player whose dad was a very wealthy industrialist from Pittsburgh. He's offered the kid his whole empire when he quits the factory, but the kid wants to go to New York and try his hand at jazz. He goes. He finds that all the time he's spent away from jazz has killed any talent he had for the horn."

Boy, *that* was nowhere near the movie that was on the screen. The casting alone sunk that boat before it left the dock.

"Once again the suits interfered with disastrous results. As the hot college kid we had a young New York actor, burning with talent, John Garfield. On *Second Chorus*, our college kids were two trumpet players, Fred Astaire, over 45, and Burgess Meredith, not much under 45. As a young secretary, Paulette Goddard in her thirties. Stick in Artie Shaw and his band, play a big number like Benny's *Sing Sing Sing*, and see how it turns out. Typical Hollywood butchery. It was an awful film"

Badly. It stunk.

"End of Hollywood and me. They didn't even have a script most of the time. They'd just ask us to wing dialogue."

Well, on the bright side, you got one of your most requested pieces *Concerto for Clarinet*.

"That's less a concerto than a bunch of pieces pasted together, ending with *Sing Sing Sing* tom toms. It was very popular everywhere we appeared. As a musician once came to me and said, "Artie, aren't you ever afraid you'll miss the Top C note at the end?" I said to him, "Put your hand on the table. Lift your index finger—were you afraid you'd miss?" The man said, "You mean it's like that?" I said, "If it's not don't mess with it."

Movies were bad, how were you with the mob? They controlled most of the places you played, nightclubs, theaters, record studios, movies—and just about everything. They drove Louis Armstrong and many musicians to exile in Europe.

"I don't know why, but they left me alone. Once I had a tiny nibble, but I made a call and never heard anything again. I was mob free."

How about drugs?

"Tough subject. I didn't touch 'em, and tried to hire guys that didn't need drugs. But after the war, in that 1945-48 period, in the era of Bird, Pres, Coltrane, Miles, Bud Powell, Lady Day, drugs were a big problem. Everyone used them."

"I still don't know how musicians can play so well when filled with heroin and coke. How did Bird invent a whole new approach and kill himself in drugs. I don't know. I don't think I could play if filled with drugs. I can't imagine how I could manage a note."

What's the best clarinet playing you did?

"The last ten bars of *These Foolish Things*—it was as close to perfect as I could get."

At that point I thought I heard an exit line. We had been talking for 3 hours. I told my boxing stories, Shaw told me all about Shaw. I had one more question.

If you had to write an epitaph what should it be?

"*He did the best he could with what he had.* But I have changed that."

To what?

"*Go Away.*"

So, Artie, thanks a lot, I'll go away and leave you alone.

# THE END

# After the Interview
# Epilogue

As I flew back to Miami I determined that I should write the conversation up before approaching senility erased most of it. I cursed Shaw for not letting me tape it.

It's not that Shaw revealed any bombshell, not heretofore reported. He was not a part in the CIA conspiracy to kill Castro. He had nothing to do with the Kennedy assassinations. He had not screwed Lupe Velez before she raped Gary Cooper, but married Tarzan.

The thing that filtered out, as I wrote down everything that was said, was a startling fact.

I was so taken with the Artie Shaw business because, gulp, I was a mirror image of Artie Shaw. I didn't think he was eccentric. Everything he did had a perfectly sound reason. If not to the public, at least to Shaw.

Take walking out of the band business at the height of his fame, when he was making the unheard sum of $26,000 a week. But he was 26-years old. He'd worked so hard to get to be the very best, yet, when he achieved just what he set out to do, it reared back and exploded in his face. Jitterbugs (his fans) didn't come to hear him play, they came to scream at the top of their lungs from start to finish. They didn't come to *hear* Shaw, they came to *see* Shaw. His introduction into the Artie Shaw thing. Papers said he was high strung. Put yourself in his patent-leather slippers.

You've worked so hard to be the best, and *because* you are the best, the public rewards you with a night long standing ovation, and no one hears your music.

It's enough to have a nervous breakdown over. Benny Goodman, a more sanguine, practical man, faced with the same thing, would simply stop the band in mid-performance, and wait for the din to subside, then he read the riot act to the kids. "If you keep yelling, we pack up and leave. Please keep quiet, listen to our band and enjoy the music."

Sensible. Adult. A way out. But Shaw was too angry, mad, high strung. He was just worn out by instant fame.

Harry James, who gave up fame as a hot jazz trumpet man (Listen to his exceptional solo on "Sing, Sing, Sing" from the Carnegie Hall Album) to make millions playing a schmaltz nanny goat style love music to millions of lovesick GI's overseas, evaluates Shaw:

"Artie was the best pure instrumentalist, had the tightest best rehearsed band, and gave the best performance, but he just couldn't *stand* the business. For Shaw there was only the *music*, music, and when he had to accept the music-*business* he gave up, and fled. We all admired him for making his statement, but at what a cost. And, in the end, he had to come back to the *business* and learn to lump it, like all the rest of us."

Buddy Rich, a very witty man, on the Carson Show with Shaw on the couch next to him, said to Artie:

"With the excellence of your bands, and your great clarinet, why did you quit? Why did you deprive us of years of great enjoyment? Why did you make us have to do without that wonderful music?"

As Shaw was caught by surprise by the usually caustic Rich started to reply, Rich finished,

"Why didn't you stay with us, so you could share the agony and worry of all those decades we had to suffer through?"

Artie Shaw and I led similar lives. We were challenged by many separate disciplines, many differing causes, and we conquered each and had repeated success in life.

Artie left his identifying feature, the world's best clarinetist, and I left my life's identity, that of a ghetto doctor to do other things. And to do them well. We both had trouble finding our way in matrimonial waters, although I won that battle finding the right wife, happy in 31 years of matrimony. Shaw never figured it out.

And now, because of a fluke, a dream and a desire to see a life long hero, Artie Shaw, and find answers that Henry and I puzzled about, I got to write this book.

Artie was warm, charming, filled with clear memories and opinions. I appreciated his company and hospitality and left fully satisfied.

People will continue to send me Shaw sightings, I'll put them in the bulging Shaw file, and continue to listen to his wonderful records.

The quality of the music cannot be challenged because it holds up. The proof lies in the reissuing of old records, even at this late date.

In conclusion, I'm glad I went. An empty chapter in my book has been filled. I'm satisfied. Now that I know Artie Shaw I see how smart I was to follow his life.

If the reader is a jazz fan, I hope this fills all the blanks you had about Artie Shaw.

If you have more to ask Shaw, call him. I did.

"Go Away" Shaw; Epitath

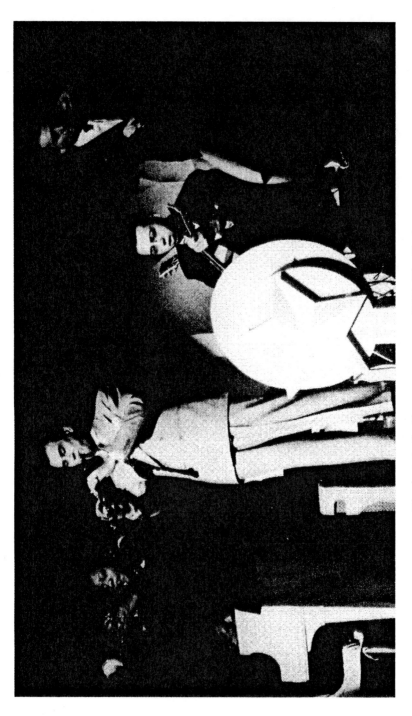

The last Artie Shaw group ever. 1954, The Embers

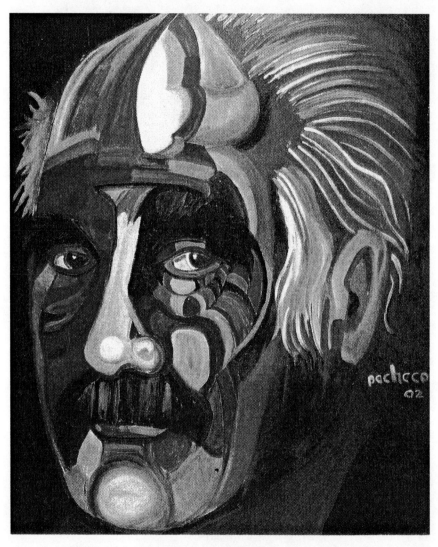

The Cubistic Shaw (94 y/o)

CPO Shaw with Navy band: Rare photo: Few exist

Back from Navy with Eliz Hearner and baby Steve

Kathleen Winsor and Artie Shaw, c. 1947

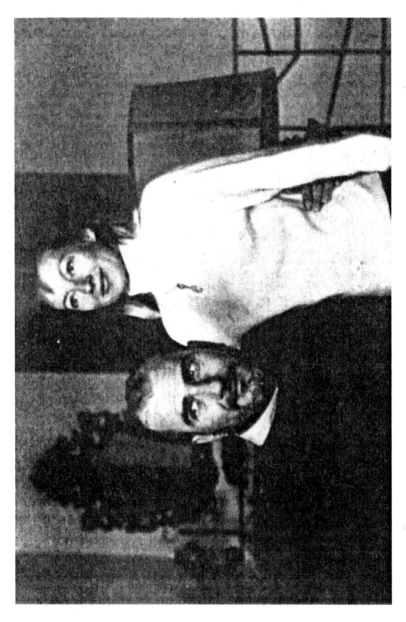

Artie Shaw and Evelyn Keyes in the home Shaw designed in Spain, late 1950s

It's easy to leave Lana, if you have Ava waiting in the wings.

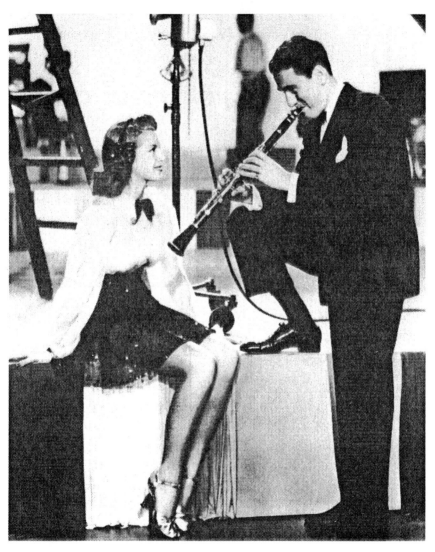

Lana and Artie appear in Dancing Coeds: They hated each other

MGM starlet in early twenties.  Lana Turner

Evelyn Keyes: 1946
Shaw's last wife

*Ferdie Pacheco*

The big string bands of the forties proved to be too expensive

Benny Goodman, King of Swing. 1938

Shaw 1939, King of Swing

The '39 band which Shaw abandoned at the Park Theatre

Artie Shaw in the moviess. 1940

Author at 13 – Heart break at the Park Theatre, 1939

Author at Art Exhibit

# PACHECO'S DISCOGRAPHY

\* A Pacheco Favorite

## 1938-39 BAND

| | |
|---|---|
| 024079-1\*Begin the Beguine | BB 7746, AXM2-5517 |
| 024080-1\*Indian Love Call | N/A |
| 024081-2 Coming On | BB 7772 |
| 024082-2\*Back Bay Shuffle | BB 7529 |
| 024083-1\*Any Old Time | N/A |
| 024084-2 I Can't Believe That You're In Love With Me | BB 7772 |

## 1939

| | |
|---|---|
| 031491\*Lover Come Back To Me | BB 10126 |
| 031492\*My Heart Stood Still | BB 10125 |
| 031493\*Rosalie | BB 10126 |
| 031494 Supper Time | BB 10127 |
| 031495 Vilia | BB 10128 |

## 1939

| | |
|---|---|
| 031864\*Alone Together | BB 10148 |
| 031865\*Rose Room | N/A |
| 031866 I Want My Share of Love | BB 10134 |
| 031867 It's All Your Fault | BB 10141 |
| 031 68 This Is It | N/A |
| 031 69 Delightful Delirium | BB 10134 |

## March 1939

| | |
|---|---|
| 032961\*Any Old Time | Vc 201575 AXM2-5533 |
| 032962\*I'm In Love With The Honorable So and So | N/A |
| 032963\*Prosschai | N/A |
| 032964\*Deep Purple | BB 10178 |
| 032999 You Grow Sweeter as the Years Go By | N/A |
| 035300\*You're So Indifferent | BB 10215 |
| 05301 Snug As A Bug In A Rug | N/A |
| 05302 If You Ever Change Your Mind | BB 10195 |
| 05303\*One Night Stand | BB 10202 |
| 0504\*One Foot In The Groove | N/A |

## June 1939

| | |
|---|---|
| 036237*Octaroon | BB 10319 AMX25533 |
| 036238*I Poured My Heart Into A Song | N/A |
| 036239 When Winter Comes | N/A |
| 036241 Out Of Nowhere | BB 10320 |
| 036240 All I Remember Is You | BB 10319 |
| 036269*Serenade To A Savage | BB 10385 |
| 036291 Easy To Say | BB 10345 |
| 036292 I'll Remember | N/A |
| 036293*Moonray | BB 10334 |
| 036294 Melancholly Mood | N/A |

## "Dancing Coed" film sound track

*Nightmare (theme)
*Non stop Flight
*Traffic Jam
*Jungle Drums
Gangbusters
*Back Bay Shuffle
*One Foot in the Grove
*At Sundown

## Café Rouge 1939

| | |
|---|---|
| Oh You Crazy Moon | HSR 176, HBCD 502 |
| *At Sundown | Vic LPT 6000 |
| Maria, My Own | Vic LPT 6000 |
| *Moonray (VHF) | Vic LPT 6000 |
| *I Can't Give You Anything But Love | HSR 176, 401 HBCD 502 |
| *El Rancho Grande (vTP) | Vic LPT 6000 |
| *What's New | HSR 176, 401 |
| *You're Mine You | HBCD 502, HSR 149 |
| *Over the Rainbow | HSR 176 |
| 043367-1*I Didn't Know What Time It Was | BB 10502 |
| 043369 Do I Love You | BB 10509 |
| *You're Mine You | - ASC-11 |
| *Serenade To A Savage | SoS 126, ASC-11 |

| | |
|---|---|
| Diga Diga Doo | Vic LPT 6000 |
| Lilac In The Rain | HSR 149, HBCD 502 |
| *My Blue Heaven | Vic LPT 6000 |
| Everything Is Jumpin' | HSR 176 |

## 1940-42 Artie Shaw with Strings

| | |
|---|---|
| *Frenesi | Vic 26542, AXM2 5556 |
| *Adios, Marquita Linda | Vic____ |
| *Gloomy Sunday | Vic 26563 |
| *My Fantasy | Vic 26614 |
| A Deserted farm | Vic____ |
| Don't fall Asleep | Vic 26563 |

## Artie Shaw Hollywood 1940

| | |
|---|---|
| Dreaming Out Loud | Vic 26642 AXM2-5556 |
| Now We Know | N/A |
| *Mister Meadowlark | Vic 26614 |
| *April in Paris | Vic 26654 |
| King For A Day | N/A |
| *Concerto for Clarinet | AFRS BMI HEPCD19 |

## Artie Shaw Gramercy Five 1940

Billy Butterfield (Trumpet), John Guarnieri (Harpsichord), Al Hendrickson (Guitar), Jud deNant (Base), Nick Fatool (Drums)

| | |
|---|---|
| 055061-1*Special Delivery Stomp | Vic 26762 |
| 055062-1*Summit Ridge Drive | Vic 26763 |
| 055063-1*Keeping Myself For You | Vic 26762 |
| 055064-1*Cross Your Heart | Vic 26763 AXM-2-5572 |

## Artie Shaw Hollywood October 1940

| | |
|---|---|
| *Love of My Life | Vic 26790 |
| A Handful Of Stars | N/A |
| *Stardust | Vic 27230 |
| Marinella | Vic 27362 |
| Danza Lucumi | Vic 27354 |

## Hollywood 1940

| | |
|---|---|
| If It's You | Vic 26760 |
| *Temptation | Vic 27230 |
| *Chantez Les bar | Vic 27354 |
| *This Is Romance | Vic 27343, AXM2-5572 |
| What Is There To Say? | Vic 27342 |
| *Pyramid | Vic 27343 |
| You Forgot About Me | Vic 27236 |
| *Who's Excited | Vic 27385 |
| Prelude in C Major | Vic 27432 |

## Gramercy Five 1940 Hollywood

| | |
|---|---|
| *Dr. Livingston I Presume | Vic 27289 |
| *When The Quails Come back To San Quentin | N/A |
| *My Blue heaven | Vic 27432 |
| *Smoke Gets In Your Eyes | Vic 27335 |

## Artie Shaw's Orchestra in NYC Victor Studio Sessions

| | |
|---|---|
| Confessing | CAL 584 AXM 2-5576 |
| Love Me A Little | Vic 27509 |
| *This Time The Dream's On Me | Vic 27609 |
| *Blues In The Night | Vic 27609 |
| Nocturne | Vic 27664 |
| *Rocking Chair | Vic 27703 |
| If I Love Again | Vic 27764 |
| Take Your Shoes Off, Baby | Vic 27719 |
| Just Kidding Around | Vic 27806 |

## NYC 1941

| | |
|---|---|
| *To A Broadway Rose | Vic 27838 |
| *St. James Infirmary Part I | Vic 27895 |
| St James Infirmary Part II | Vic 27895 |
| *Deuces Wild | Vic 27838 |
| *Someone's Rocking My Dreamboat | Vic 27746 |
| Suite #8 | Vic 280405 |

## Artie 1942

| | |
|---|---|
| *Hindustan | Vic 27798 |
| Not Mine | Vic 27799 |
| Somebody Nobody Loves | Vic 27798 |
| Carnival | Vic 27860 |
| Needlenose | Vic 27860 |
| *Two In One Blues | Vic 27860 |
| *Sometimes I Feel Like A Motherless Child | Vic 27806 |

**Artie Shaw disbanded, married** Eliz Kern and joined the U.S. Navy. This band, made up of excellent musicians did not record one side.

For the record, the band was comprised of Frank Beach, John Best, Conrad Grozzo, Max Kaminsky (Trumpets). Tasso Harris, Dick LeFavre, Tak Takvoriant (Trombones) Mack Pierce, Ralph LeFollet, Sam Donahue, Joe Aglora (Sax, Reeds) Harold Wax (Piano, Accordian) Rocky Coluccio (Piano) Al Hovesh (Guitar) Barney Speiler (Base) Dave Tough (Drums).

## 1944-45 Post War: Hollywood Band featuring Roy Eldridge

| | |
|---|---|
| *Ac-Cent-Uate The Positive | Vic 20-1612 |
| *Lady Day | Vic 20-1620 |
| *Jumpin' On The Merry-go-round | Vic 20-1612 |
| *I'll Never Be The Same | Vic 20-1638 |
| *Can't Help Loving That Man | Vic 20-1931 |
| *S' Wonderful | Vic 20-1638 |
| *Bedford Drive | Vic 20-1969 |

## With Gramercy Five

| | |
|---|---|
| 0032-4*The Grabtown Grapple | Vic 20-1647 |
| 0033-4*The Sad Sack | N/A |

NOTE: Grabtown was the hometown of wife Ava Gardner.

## Hollywood 1945

| | |
|---|---|
| *But Not For Me | Vic 20-1745 |
| Tea For Two | Vic PM 42403 |
| *Summertime | Vic LPM 1648, AXM2-5579 |

| | |
|---|---|
| *Easy To Love | Vic 20-1934 |
| Time On My Hands | Vic 20-1930 |
| Tabu | Vic 1696 |

## 1945 in Los Angeles

| | |
|---|---|
| 1059-1*A Foggy Day | Vic 20-1933 |
| 1060-1*The Foolish Things | Vic 20-1930 |
| 1061-1 Lucky Number | AXM2-5580 |
| 1062-1*You Go To My Head | AXM2-5579 |
| 1062-1*The Man I Love | AXM2-5579 |
| 1068-1  *I Could Write A Book | Vic 20-1933 |
| 1061-3  Lucky Number | Vic 20-1937 |
| 1069-1  Thrill of a Lifetime | Vic 20-1937 |
| 10543  Kasbah | Vic 20-1932 |
| 1070-1*Love Walked In | Vic 20-1745 |
| 1070-1*Soon | Vic 20-1742 |
| 10721  Keeping Myself for You | Vic 20 1936 |
| 10731  No One But You | Vic LPV 582 |
| 1075-1 That's For Me | Vic 20-1716 |
| 1076-2*They Can't Take That Away | Vic 20-1743 |
| 1079-1*Our Love Is Here To Stay | N/A |
| 1080-1*I Was Doing All Right | Vic 20-1742 |
| 1081-1  Someone To Watch Over Me | Vic 20-1744 |
| 1101-1*Maid With The Flaccid Air | Vic 28-0406, AXM25580 |
| 1089-1 They Didn't Believe Me | Vic 20-1931, AM2 5580 |
| 1090-1*Dancing On The Ceiling | Vic LPT 1020 |
| 1091-1*I Can't Get Started | Vic 20-1934 |
| 1097-1*Don't Blame Me | AMX2-5580 |
| 1098-1 Yolanda | Vic 20-1716 |
| 1047-2*But Not For Me | N/A |
| 1099-1 I Can't Escape From You | Vic 20-1936 |
| 1104-1*Mysterious | Vic 20-1800 |
| 1105-1 Hop, Skip, and Jump | Vic 20-1800 |
| 5544*You Do Something To Me | MUS 391 MVS 503 |
| 5547*In The Still Of The Night | MUS 390 |
| 5546*My Heart Belongs To Daddy | MUS 392 |
| 55431*Night And Day | MUS 389 AFJ 248 |

| | |
|---|---|
| 55481*What Is This Thing Called Love? | MUS 390 AFJ 248 |
| 5541*I've Got You Under M' Skin | MUS 392 (Torme) |
| 5542*Get Outta Town | MUS 389 (Torme) |
| 5629*For You, For Me, Forevermore | MUS 412 |
| 5636*Love For Sale | MUS 391 |
| 5647*They Can't Convince Me | MUS 441 |
| 5650 And So, To Bed | MUS 441 |
| 5651 Connecticut | MUS 445 |
| 5702 It's The Same Old Dream | MUS 492 |
| 5703 I Believe | N/A |
| 5704 When You're Around | MUS 512 |

**Artie Shaw** retired from performing completely during 1947 and 1948, devoting himself to writing books and developing as a classical clarinetist.

**1949** Much of Shaw's time was taken up with classical, experimental jazz, re-recording of old favorites, etc. I am not interested in this phase of Shaw but only in commercial music pieces, so I won't list the few records he made as a classical clarinetist.

### Shaw and the New 1950 Gramercy Five

Don Fagerquist (Trumpet), GI Barrios (Piano), Jimmy Rainey (Guitar), Dick Niverson (Base), Irv Kluger (Drums), Artie Shaw (Clarinet).

| | |
|---|---|
| *Summit Ridge Drive | TTI 564-65 Sol 509 |
| *Grabtown Grapple | "            " |
| *Smoke Gets In Your Eyes | "            " |
| Pied Piper Theme | "            " |
| *Cross Your Heart | "            " |
| 75677 There Must Be Something Better Than Love | De 24870 Ajaz 291 |
| 75678 Nothing From Nothing | N/A |
| 75674*Love Walked In | De 24869 Ajaz 291 |
| 75880*So Easy | De DL 74462 |
| 76081*Continental | De 27056 |
| 76082*I'll Remember April | N/A |
| 76079 He's Gone Away | De 27009 Ajaz 291 |
| *Foggy Foggy Day | Ajaz 298 |

| | |
|---|---|
| 76099 Crumbum  (Gramercy Five) | De 27196 Ajaz 298 |
| 76100 Shekomeko Shuffle (Gramercy Five) | |

## The Decca Years

| | |
|---|---|
| 76197 Count Every Star | De 27042 Ajaz 298 |
| 76197 If You Were Only Mine | N/A |
| 76426*I'm Forever Blowing Bubbles | De 27186 |
| 76427*You're Mine you | N/A |
| 76669*Don't Worry About Me | De 27213 |
| 76670 Blue Again | N/A |
| 76671 It's A Long Way To Tipperary | N/A |
| 76672*Show Me The Way To Go Home | N/A |

## 1953

84799*These Foolish Things
84800*In The Still Of The Night
84801*That Old Black Magic
84802*I'll Be Seeing You
84817*It Could Happen To You
84818*They Can't Take That Away From Me
84819*All The Things You Are
84820*September Song

## New 1945 Gramercy Five

Roy Eldridge (Trumpet), Dodo Marmarosa (Piano), Barney Kesse (Guitar), Morris Rayman (Base), Lou Fromm (Drums)

| | |
|---|---|
| 1102-1 Scuttlebutt | Vic 20-1929 |
| 1103-1 The Gentle Grifter | Vic 20-1929 |

## Big Band

| | |
|---|---|
| 5408 Let's Walk | MUS 357 MVS 503 |
| 5416 Love Of My Life | MUS 378 MVS CD 51 |
| 5417*Ghost Of A Chance | MUS 357 |
| 5418*How Deep Is The Ocean | MUS 409 |
| 5419 The Glider | MUS CD-50 |
| 5420 The Hornet | MUS 408-MUS CD-51 |

## The Musicraft Years

Shaw disbanded in November 1945. Shaw did not have another regular working unit until 1949.

During 1946, Shaw did not have a regular touring unit. He convened studio bands for recording work for a new label, Musicraft.

5473 I Got The Sun In The Morning:               MUS 365
5474 Along With Me
Shaw began featuring Mel Torme and the Meltones.

For historians, records of this 1953-54 episode are divided into two groups. The first group with the Bop musicians was recorded in New York while they played at the Embers, late February-early March 1954.

| | |
|---|---|
| *The Sad Sack | MGC 159, MGV 2014 |
| | Ajaz 431, BOMR 71-7715, |
| | MM 65071-2 |
| *I've Got A Crush On You | MM 65101 |
| The Chaser | Ajaz 440 |
| *Tenderly | MGC-160 |
| Sunny Side Up | Ajaz 446, MM 65119-2 |
| *Autumn Leaves | MGC-645, SoS 125, Ajaz 440 |
| *Dancing In The Dark | MM 65101-2 |
| *Someone To Watch Over Me | MM 65071-2 |
| Stop and Go Mambo | Ajaz 446, MM 65101-2 |
| Besame Mucho | MM 65101-2 |
| *Grabtown Grapple | MGV 2015 MM 65101-2 |
| *I Can't Get Started | MM 655071-2 |
| *Begin The Beguine | MM 65101-2 |
| *Don't Take Your Love From Me | N/A |
| *Cross Your Heart | N/A |
| *How High The Moon | N/A |
| *Stardust | N/A |
| *Summit Ridge Drive | N/A |
| *Scuttlebutt | N/A |
| *Frenesi | N/A |

After October, Kluger came in to anchor the group in the 'old Shaw' style.

The group recorded his last commercial records in June 1954 in Hollywood. This group was comprised of five modern soloists:
Hank Joseph (Piano), Joe Puma (Guitar), Tommy Potter (Base), Irv Kluger (Drums), Artie Shaw (Clarinet).

Rough Riders                 Clef MGC 630, Ajaz 451 RWJ-1001
My Funny Valentine
*Dancing On The Ceiling
*Too Marvelous
 Yesterdays
 S'posin'
*Bewitched, Bothered and Bewildered
*September Song                              MM 65101-2

**Final Note:**
Shaw said that around 1948-9, he was called to form an L.A. band of the best musicians in town. He went out and found the best of the Bop Boys. "They were brilliant musicians. As a band, it was the best I had. But discipline was a major problem. In that period, drugs were the major problems."

Shaw bands had the reputation of being the best-disciplined bands. Shaw stood for no hard drugs.

"That band could blow you off the stand some nights; other nights they might not show up. It was chaos. I had to disband."

# Artie Shaw: A Brief Biography

Artie Shaw's mother, Sarah Strauss from Austria had married Harry Arshawsky, from Russia after they had immigrated to New York City. Artie Shaw was born May 23rd, 1910.

Shaw grew up in a climate of continual down hill economic failure. His father worked as a dressmaker, then as a photographer. Both businesses failed, and eventually they moved to New Haven Connecticut. It proved to be the first encounter with anti-Semitism. Shaw recalls the most memorable experience of that time was a near-death experience of near drowning.

"I saw the light, heard the music, everything. Then they started me up again. I always thought it was a hallucination."

Around the age of 13 Shaw started studying the piano, and saw the profession of music as a serious way of making a living.

Shaw's life took an important turn when he convinced his father that he should take up the saxophone. The instrument required $40 which Shaw earned and saved to buy. It was a C-melody saxophone, roughly between the tenor and alto sax in size and quality although appearing similar to an undersized tenor.

Shaw, because of his obvious musical talent worked his way up the Regional New England and New York orchestras of that day. He was still very shy, and was prone to letting his horn make his statement.

Rudi Valley (in his book "My Time is Your Time") remembered the shy withdrawn musician like this "A young Jewish boy of rather sullen demeanor, who had little or nothing to say about himself or his dogged study of the saxophone."

During these early days, with success following success, he decided to change his name. He changed it to a plainer Art Shaw. This killed two birds with one stone, it was convenient and it helped him avoid issues about being Jewish.

By 1927-8 he was not only well known as a studio musician who had taught himself to sight read. While with Joe Cantor, he decided to try arranging for the band. He was also successful there. He was in demand as a sideman in all the orchestras of that day.

After several successful years with bands like Austin Wylie and Irving Aaronson, Shaw reached an important crossroads. Shaw decided if he were to become a star instrumentalist he had to choose one instrument. Luckily he chose the clarinet.

At the height of his popularity, Shaw recorded classical music. One day in Chicago, he heard an exciting piece of music. Long hair music was decried by jazz musicians who didn't have the musical sophistication to appreciate what they heard. Shaw did.

The piece that set Shaw on fire was Stravinsky's "Firebird Suite" Shaw claims he was knocked for a loop and rushed to the salesman and asked,

"Do you have anything else like this?"

"You mean the same composer?"

"Yes anything. I'll take it all."

Artie Shaw went home with Stravinsky's "Le Sacre du Printemps," the complete "Firebird Suite" and a Debussy "l'Apres-midi d'un faun."

This discovery affected his writing and arranging of music. Musicians of that day resented the new long hair invasion and found the music deeply incomprehensible. A serious study of his discography how he stuck to the music, and how many were based on operetta, e.g., "Deeply Within a Morning Sunrise" and serious composition such as "Maid with a Flaccid Air."

In New York, 1930, just as the young man was poised at the starting line in his musical life with a reputation, fame and a steady girlfriend, tragedy struck to derail the Shaw express to fame and fortune. To start his father died just as he arrived in New York.

The news stories stated under the headline, "Car Kills a Man, Pair Held." The story read, Artie Shaw and Bette Goldstein, 19 of hotel Marseilles in a car with Ohio license plates, struck and killed a pedestrian, George Woods, age 60, a chef on a yacht on Broadway and 91st street. The car drove on but witnesses took the license number, and the police, found the couple in their car on Columbus Avenue shortly afterward. It was reported that Shaw stated that he thought he had hit a traffic stanchion.

The six months that followed were the worst of his long life. He had to leave the Aaronson band, he spent all the money he had saved, and in desperation had to move back in with his mother in New York. Union regulations required that Shaw could be granted a Union Local 802 card after six months. He couldn't sleep and he walked the streets day and night or rode the subway to and fro. For all the lucky breaks of his early life, he had now reached rock bottom. Only one thing was left to bring him lower: <u>he could go to jail</u>.

Hanging over his head was the possibility of 5 -to-10 year sentence for vehicular homicide and leaving the site of an accident.

The law must have been much more lenient in that day, how he beat the rap I'll never know. It cost him all he had, and plenty of future money, but Shaw walked. When he returned to the band it was with a profound relief, and new found joy at creating new music, and playing it superbly.

## Willy the Lion Smith

New York: A new life started for the beaten down 19 year old musician. He had experienced strange adventures, rubbed up against derelicts, the night people, and the dangerous. But, true to his tough inner self, he managed to abstract good from evil. For music was always his life, his savior. And on the streets of Harlem, music was a 24 hour life raft. There Shaw found William Lion Smith the legendary jazz piano man.

Shaw reminisced:

"Willy worked every night from 12 to 6. He packed a little cellar joint in Harlem, named Pod and Jerry's.

After Willy spotted my white face, backed up to a corner of the piano, one white face amidst a sea of black, he befriended me. 'This ofay got to be a musician, ain't nobody dumb enough to risk his life coming in here and less'n he a jazzman.'

After that, I felt that this tiny joint, with its dim light, small bar at the end of the room, it's sprinkling of red checkered tables, was so what I'd been looking for. For the first time during that desperately unhappy period, I felt safe, at home here. If Willy the Lion adopted you, everybody loved you. I was home. Safe!

But the main thing was the music! Willie the Lion could play jazz! Man, he dominated the jazz piano player. He was king!

The Lion was, I now know, one of the very few "originals." From a purely harmonic standpoint, no one could reach him!

Willy the Lion, a generous man, wrote in his autobiography "Music On My Mind" about the young Shaw.

"For several months a young handsome clarinet player named Artie Shaw would bring his clarinet and play along with me. I wouldn't let just anyone join us he had to have serious chops. Shaw just had to get to New York he got hisself in deep trouble. Aside from the local 802 didn't let you play for dough anywhere in New York for six months. Man, those were hungry times for the kid. But night after night, there he was, suit all pressed, shaved clean and handsome as a movie star. I didn't say nuttin, I jus' listened. The boy could play.

My boy Artie was a good student and the Lion was proud of him when I'd take him with me out to jam at the after hour sessions we had with the Big Boys."

Shaw responded:

"Playing with Lion was a brand new experience... and I would do my best to get with it, until after a while I began to get the drift, to latch out to what Lion was doing to the point where I could have a general predictability of where we would end up.

After hours they would play at Goldgraben's Blind Pig until they couldn't stay awake. For Shaw it was exhilarating. One night the great Barney Brigard the clarinet star of Harlem sat listening to Shaw accompanying the Lion.

"Say Lion, who is the musician? Asked Barney pointing to Shaw with a cigar.

"Artie Shaw. He play with me every night!"

"Humph"...he grunted, "He is a good Blues Man."

The Lion said that he was. Shaw drifted out on a cloud all the way home.

When his union card came in, Shaw flew up town where he was in heavy demand. On one show Shaw remembered, they had a gig at Princeton. The band was formidable including Bix Beiderbeck, saxes Eddie Miller, Tommy Dorsey, Artie, and Bunny Berigen. Lennie Haydon, who later married Lena Horn, sat in on piano. What a band that must've been!

During these hectic years of the early 30's, Shaw found time to elope with Jane Carns, daughter of a doctor in Ashtabula, Ohio. The bride was not quite of age and the irate father had the marriage annulled. Shaw didn't count that as a marriage.

In 1933 Shaw was showing all of his unhappiness of the band business. He did what he was destined to do all his adult life. He quit flat. Out. Gone. He bought a farm in Bucks County and started to write and novel on Bix Beiderbeck. Try as he might, he found out that he was that he was a superb clarinetist and a lousy novelist.

Hear Shaw in "The Trouble with Cinderella"

"All I knew was I didn't know anything. I was obsessed with a sense of my own, abysmal ignorance. A week or so later I moved back to New York and started to figure out how to fill the large gaps in my education. On the other hand, since I have not touched a clarinet or tenor sax in a year, I now had a hard time producing a musical sound. Since these were the only tools by which I could make a living and pay for further education, I was in a tough place."

Notwithstanding that dire forecast, Shaw jumped right back in and recorded and played radio, studio, and concert gigs through 1934-35.

By 1935 he started to formulate an ambitious plan to form his own band. He was ready.

## The "Interlude in B Flat" Bombshell.

During 1936 Shaw decided to participate in the world's first swing concert. The event was organized by Joe Helbock of the Onyx Club. Shaw was asked to participate by playing a 3 to 5 minute interval with a small group performance while the stage was being changed.

Shaw, always an original thinker decided to offer "something just a tiny bit different." He was certainly different since the program was filled with big bands and jazz combos.

Shaw appeared onstage in front of group: string quartet, clarinet, and a piano-less rhythm section. Since Shaw had written it in B flat, and since it was meant to be an interlude, Shaw called it "Interlude in B flat." Shaw had his whimsical moments.

The concert took place at the Imperial Theater on West 45th Street on May 24th, 1936, one day after Shaw's 26th birthday. Shaw, confident and cool started up the piece. The public was shocked

The audience made up of primarily musicians, people in the music business, and hard  jazz fans was overwhelmed. Leonard Feather, top jazz critic wrote: Artie's number one, Interlude in B Flat flat, broke up the show. They asked for an encore but Shaw had only written one piece, so he coolly played it again, to an even bigger applause! Artie Shaw, in what was to become a habit with him, became #1 Talk of the Town he had finally arrived.

Shaw wasted no time when opportunity knocked. He had played around arranging and writing for that format and he had the musicians he wanted.  So he quickly signed up to a major concert featuring 17 bands and a Broadway theater was rented to accommodate the important Swing Concert. Wingy Manone and Stuff Smith kicked it off with an excellent small combo swing. Next came Shaw. From the review of that day:

"Next came Artie Shaw and his swing string ensemble, which stole a show."

"The combo consisting of a legit string section plus a rhythm section, and featuring Artie Shaw's clarinet…He has what is possibly the only new creation in modern music within the past five years. Arrangements by Shaw were distinctly outstanding. Intro into the first selection, which was probably original, had a force bar string playing sustained harmonics a la Debussy and Ravel ("La Valse"). Then came a fanfare rhythm.  Shaw came in for dynamic clarinet work.  That will probably keep Goodman up all night. Absolutely masterful on technique and tone.  Shaw now rates with Goodman any day."

Shaw formed his first permanent commercial band, hired Peg La Centra to sing, and got a great booking at the Lexington. He also hired and old pal Tony Pastor to sing novelty tunes, as well as play tenor.

After a few months the management complained bitterly that the orchestra wasn't drawing the public as it should. Shaw faced in enraged manager:

An irate manager screamed at Shaw:

"You are talking about music. I don't give a god dam about music. I'm paying you to play so I can get customers in the joint and make some dough. What the hell do you think I'm running here a goddamn concert hall?

If you want to take your pants down on the bandstand every night, and take a crap every night, and if people will pay to see you take a crap up there every night, then I'll pay you!

That's how much I give a Goddamn about what kind of music you play."

At this point Artie Shaw woke up. He wasn't in the music business. He was in the entertainment business!

Badly shaken by this realization, he nonetheless continued to receive the critical raves of his with peers. One night a young girl sat through two sets, then came back stage to see him.

She was perky, pretty and oh, so young. "Hi, I'm Judy Garland. I'm a singer at MGM; I just had to tell you how great your music is!"

"How old are you?" The pleased Shaw asked. When she told him 14, he hugged her in delight.

"Do you realize that nobody but musicians like what we're doing?" Shaw marveled that a girl so young should have an ear and perception to appreciate such music.

For the next year of this 'advanced' band featuring Peg La Centra and Tony Pastor played the big hotels and clubs. Shaw did not feel the acceptance he felt was due to the band.

The band evoked its era, but it was conceded to be 'advanced.' It was apparent Shaw knew what he wanted and got it jazz-oriented dance with new tone colors in superior taste. He did this without compromise to his musical integrity by arranging popular material to the level of art while supplying genuine exciting jazz.

Shaw disbanded the group as a result of public apathy.

In March of 1937, a momentous event occurred in music which turned Shaw around caused him to form his "loud" band. Swing arrived with a Bang! Benny Goodman appeared at the Carnegie Hall Swing Concert. His band playing at the Paramount caused riots. Benny was crowned King of Swing.

## The Beginning

By April 1937, Shaw had organized his new band, the "loud band", minus the soothing strings, and appeared at the Raymor Ballroom in Boston.

Although the new bands boasted new Shaw arrangements, excellent first-class musicians, and a dedication necessary to succeed but he was always short of dates, short of cash. Not yet widely accepted.

Shaw got lucky again. He came into the sight of Si Shribman, who with his brother Charlie, booked bands and who operated a ballroom chain of 20 ballrooms. Goodman was getting nervous about Shaw's rising reputation as a clarinetist and leader.

Sir Shribman made the Shaw band the pet project. He got them jobs, loaned or advanced money when things got short, and was the band's principal fan. Shaw said he loved Si not only for the way he guided them, but also because of the quiet gentlemanly way in which he treated them. He was a rare manager, and a rare man. At last, Shaw was happy!

Artie Shaw had a consummate good luck to get Max Kaminsky, a great jazz soloist, and first trumpet, and the darkly beautiful giant of female of jazz singers, Billie Holiday. With the driven direction of Si Shribman, the band played everywhere. They had come together as Shaw had wanted, and now, they widely accepted and in demand. Unfortunately in racist America, a black singer did not fit in with a white band. Billy had to go, and she did. She fled from the all white Shaw band, mourned by every musician the band.

And, then it happened "Begin the Beguine". The band exploded!

# Begin the Beguine

With everything going Shaw's way he inadvertently stepped on a diamond in the rough.

Tommy Dorsey and Benny Goodman were recorded in on RCA Victor Black label, selling for 75¢ a disk. Shaw was relegated Bluebird for 35¢ a record, the cheaper public label of Victor. The studio network executives called for a first record or an up-tempo band favorite, "The Indian Love Call", which featured a jump vocal by Tony Pastor. That was the A side designed to sell the record. The B record was relegated to Artie Shaw's choice.

There are as many fathers to "Begin the Beguine" as there were great musicians in Shaw's band. A simplification by Shaw is this: Max Kaminsky, the trumpet man, stated "One day I was noodeling around with this tune and Shaw told me to put it down on paper, Shaw got hold of it and with Jerry Gray and Chuck Petersen worked up a rhythmic approach that never made it. Jerry Grey, a great arranger came in the next day with the introduction that was very catchy. Shaw stopped the band after a few minutes and said, "Let's do it in 4-4 time." So we changed the time, but kept Jerry Gray cords.

They tried it for the first time at Roseland and the crowd went wild. It was a big hit!

"When I went over that reported version of the origins of "Begin the Beguine" Shaw just shrugged, "Everyone wants to get into the act."

Eventually they weakened.

On that same session Victor included three excellent Shaw compositions: "Coming On", "Back Bay Shuffle" "Any old-time". On this last track Shaw brought back Billie Holiday to record it. Later, Shaw recorded the same tune with Helen Forrest. Holiday's is vastly superior in as much as Shaw wrote the tune specifically for her. Victor stuck with two different vocalists on one tune, chose to push Helen Forrest.

Shaw cautiously slipped "Begin the Beguine" into the book at a college date in Indiana. Wild cheering greeted the number as it started, then finished. Shaw thought someone had done something spectacular on the dance floor. The number was requested again. Wild cheering followed, louder this time.

"Looks like we got a hit, boys," said Shaw.

On October 28, 1938 Shaw brought his excited band to the Blue Room of the hotel Lincoln. The Lincoln was a cold room, deaf for bands. This time Shaw was so sure of his band that he signed for long-term engagement. The best part was that the Lincoln carried an NBC radio hookup and a hot band would be broadcasting nightly coast to coast. Shaw was ecstatic. Shaw remembers:

"Opening night there was a madhouse. From there on I couldn't think straight. Photographers from Life, the New York tabloids, and autograph hunters that were vicious, everything all at once, plus all kinds of disagreeable and unexpected pressures were being put on me. We were a hit! We had it made!

Now began the era that Shaw remembers with distaste. "I lost my identity." Shaw the boy musician who wanted so badly to play good music, turned into the **Artie Shaw Thing**. I retreated back into my head, tried to put the manic **Artie Shaw Thing** back in its proper place, but it wouldn't fit, it wouldn't go away. For the rest of my life, the **Artie Shaw Thing** would always be there pushing the real Artie Shaw back into the shadows.

From the days of wild success to when Shaw took the band to California the band was besieged by fans everywhere they went. They complained of a lack of privacy.

California was golden for a while then it too turned into fan driven mania. Shaw and the band appeared in the movie "Dancing Coed" with the young landed Lana Turner. They were both young and self-absorbed, and did not get along. He fell ill in the middle of a performance, diagnosed as agranulocytosis and took months to recuperate. Little Judy Garland attended to him lovingly each day. She had a monster crush on Shaw, who looked at her as a child and focused on Bette Grable.

## Escape After Success

By the time we came back to the band he was having first thoughts of running away from the band business, which he felt was choking him to death.

Shaw recalls: "At the stage I was in then, any little thing would have been sufficient: and so because of a slight unpleasantness with some idiot on the floor, I suddenly decided I'd had it. Instead of kicking him in the teeth I walked off the bandstand, I walked up to my room and called my lawyer."

He put it in his contract with his band and when they were finished, Shaw's stepped into his Packard and left.

Shaw's relief was enormous, as he recalls:

"I got in my car and started driving. It was snowing hard, my big car had a great heater, it was warm and comforting, and I knew that that night I wouldn't have to show up in a band stand before a crowd of ogling strangers, involved in the Shaw Thing. Now, it was Artie Shaw, private citizen. It felt fine!"

Shaw ran Acapulco, A little Mexican sleepy fishing village. No one knew where he was, the entire country was looking for him.

He surfaced in the usual Shaw style. He saved the life of Ann Chapman, a debutante. She was caught in a raging undertow. Shaw fearlessly dived in to save her but in doing so broke his leg. With a broken leg and ligament damage to his knee he had to return to Los Angeles to have it treated. Artie Shaw found himself back in the spotlight.

The escape was over. Shaw much relieved and tranquilized returned with his batteries recharged, and ready to plunge in the fray once again.

# The War

When Shaw re-entered the rat race he found RCA Victor executives waiting for him. He owed the company four records. Shaw, by now, needed the money. He hastily gathered a band of top L.A. musicians. They're all stars. They started recording March 3rd, 1940.

There first choice was a fisherman's chantey that Shaw had heard every morning from his seaside villa. He arranged it, and Skitch Henderson and Claude Thornhill helped Shaw produce a masterpiece. "Frenesi" was an instant hit and sold a million records. The money came pouring in and with it came a small Mexican attorney with a brief case. Turned out it wasn't a primitive original fisherman's chant but a piece by Mexican song writer, already recorded by several Mexican bands and by Xavier Cugat. That cost Victor and Shaw $1 million. One down, and three to ago.

Undaunted, he took the All-Star orchestra back to the recording studio and produced three more records, which each sold a million copies.

Shaw loved Billy Butterfield's open full body trumpet style. He turned him loose on the beginning of "Star Dust". It became a huge hit during the war, and long time after. Beside the Butterfield startling solo it had a great Shaw musical arrangement and one Shaw's greatest clarinet solos. Contrast Shaw's beautiful solo today, with Goodman solo of that period. And you can understand what Shaw means when he says:

"Goodman plays the clarinet, I play the music."

The full orchestra with strings issued a lush, soft, "Dancing in the Dark" and a great Shaw solo made it million dollar seller.

Batting a hundred with the 3 owed records, Shaw lightened up, dug deep into his band and had a little fun with the Gramercy 5: comprised of Johnnie Guarnieri piano and harpsichord, Judd de Naur, bass. Billy Butterfield, trumpet, Nick Fatool, drums and of course the star, Artie Shaw. Another home run! Artie had hit four out of four. Another 4 million sellers. Shaw was back!

A surprise spur of the moment supper date with a gorgeous Lana Turner turned out to have surprised bombshell ending. On the first date they flew to Arizona on a dare found nothing to do in Arizona after midnight but get married. So they did.

Shaw had been serious romancing Betty Grable the No. 1 pinup of America, and she expressed surprise:

"It must have come on him very suddenly."

Judy Garland's mom called Artie told him off, ending with the quote that had broken her heart. Shaw had this to say:

"The whole business had an unreal feeling about it, even Lana, lying there next to me in bed, seemed unreal. It had happened so fast."

Judy had the last word:

"Artie, she's a beautiful girl, but it's like sitting in a room with a beautiful vase."

They were wed February 12, 1940. Four months later they divorced. Why? Shaw went off to do tour. He was informed that Lana was pregnant. He came back, adjusted to the fact that he was to be a father. He was happy.

Only in fact, he wasn't. Mr. Mayer, of MGM was furious, ordering her to abort the child, which she did. Shaw was furious. Divorce granted July 3, 1940. It didn't seem to bother Shaw lot.

During the 1940-41 period that followed Shaw reorganized a big full band, filled with top musicians, and called it the million dollar band. The band was superb.

He went into Victor studios and produced six very popular records: "This Time the Dreams on Me" written by Shaw "Blues in the Night" a superb hit featuring legendary Hot Lips Page, singing and playing his horn. That sold a million.

Of the four the original jazz instrumentalist recorded that day all were considered hits and met audience as well as critical acclaim.

The somber, but beautiful Thomas Grizelle's "Nocturne" with a special Shaw solo. "Rocking Chair" by Hoagy Carmichael, already an established jazz piece and in a mesmerizing version of Vincent Youman's "Through the Years."

Shaw was clearly back with an exclamation point. How could he guess that the "Shaw Luck" which dog him again?

In December 7, 1941 Japan attacked Pearl Harbor. Shaw, very moved, disbanded his orchestra and on March 3, 1942 he marries Eliz Kearns, daughter of the famous composer Jerome Kearns. On April 28, 1942 Shaw enlists in the U.S. Navy. He will spend the rest of the war in the Pacific theater of operations. The combat zone.

Expecting to be given the cordial welcome that the Air Force gave Glenn Miller, who had given him the Captain's commission and a carte blanche to form an Air Force Band, Artie signed up for the Navy, before he made a deal. He reasoned he was more famous than Miller and a star clarinetist.

Shaw was shocked to be treated badly. There was no officer's commission in the offing. He was put through a rough basic training without privilege or rank.

He was put directly into mine-sweeping squadron and, sent to the North Atlantic. Shaw spent a very hard few months, where he was almost developing frostbite of his fingers, which would have ended his professional life as a clarinetist. Sick with other conditions he was hospitalized for months and the naval hospital. He had come close to being a war casualty which would have ended his career. From here out, his tussles with the United States Navy were legendary. Pure Artie Shaw. He didn't give in easily.

Feeling pretty fit he asked his agent to bring him a suit of civilian clothes and his Lincoln convertible. With a purpose in mind but no fixed plan, he drove directly to the office of the Secretary the Navy, Forrestal.

He got through the elaborate security system using his famous name and his face until the he got to the last man, a crusty sea dog of a rear admiral.

"Say, aren't you Artie Shaw? And aren't you in the Navy? What are you doing in civvies? You know that carries a year the Brig? The old man was about to call the Shore Police when Shaw was saved by Forrestal, bursting through the door and hugging Shaw. Turns out he was a huge fan! Thank God for "Begin the Beguine!"

Shaw blurted out his problem. The U.S. Navy was disinterested in Shaw's offer to form a Navy Band, a la Glenn Miller. And Shaw gingerly touched upon the subject of rank. He couldn't command and orchestra without rank. The Navy balked on this, but made him a Chief Petty Officer, which rank he kept until his discharge in 1945.

He was given carte blanche to skim the best musicians in the Navy. He found his favorite old band veterans Max Kaminsky, the great first trumpet, and everybody's favorite big band drummer, Dave Tough. They both presented a problem: They were physical wrecks and old for the Navy. Shaw insisted he would be irresponsible for them.

Shaw said laughing out loud.

"I could get Kaminsky by but Dave Tough was really a wreck. His heavy drinking had wasted his body." The doctor eyed the wreck skeptically:

"I can't let this guy in the Navy I can recommend him for hospitalization."

"Do a sit up by quarters, Dave." Shaw asked of wasted Dave Tough."

Tough went through one third, pause, the mid-third, pause and then passed out unconscious from the effort of his last third sit-up. The doctor looked at Shaw and in his eyes, "Well?" Without blinking an eye Shaw said:

"He's the best brush man in the entire nation: We gotta have him."

The doctor shrugged and passed both of the men. Jazz musicians were a tough breed and crazy. The Shaw Navy Band was formed. It was great. Shaw, for once was satisfied.

After a break in period in San Francisco where his wife came to stay with him, Shaw's Navy Band 501 was ready!

## The War in the Pacific

The Artie Shaw Navy Band 501 was unofficially called The Rangers. It was, Shaw remembers, one of the best bands he ever had because it meant all first-rate pros and because of the war, they were stuck with each other for five years. Unlike his civilian bands that constantly changed musicians, this band became one voice, and that one voice was Artie Shaw. A pity that they never recorded this band like they did Glenn Miller

Things started off as swell as they broke in the band at Pearl Harbor. Shaw insisted on playing equal time for enlisted men as well as officers which made him a big hero to the men. The musicians lived in regular Navy barracks. On Monday, Wednesday and Fridays they played for enlisted personnel at the Breakers Hotel. In the evenings they played at the Officer's Club. In between they played at the advance bases scattered around the islands. Shaw, as a Chief Petty Officer was quartered in the Halekulani Hotel. Claude Thornhill stayed at a friend's apartment in Honolulu.

Claude Thornhill, Shaw's longtime friend, an ex-roommate, hit it lucky here.

Claude Thornhill an exquisite pianist, remained on the stand between sets to play. He caught admiral Chester Nimitz's ear, and he ordered Thornhill to stay behind when The Rangers left for the dangerous war zone. Shaw was happy for his old friend but lost a big chunk of the band's musicianship, for Thornhill was a master composer and arranger and Shaw's musical alter ego.

They boarded the new, slick behemoth battle wagon, the North Carolina, destined for Noumea, the Capital of New Caledonia, and a huge naval base.

It was here that Artie Shaw experienced his epiphany (as related by Shaw in the text and shown on the back cover by the author's of large oil painting.)

His reception by the entire ship's crew was so loud and sustained that Shaw came to the realization that he was not just a musician but he had become an American icon.

He was finally bigger than the "**Shaw Thing**." He and his music had a great meaning to his country and armed forces. Artie Shaw, icon, had arrived.

From Novmea The Rangers were flown out to the outlying islands to play for the wounded in hospitals, and for men recuperating from combat, waiting to refill to return to the bitter battle.

The band and Shaw were shocked by what they saw. Where piano wouldn't fit Shaw used Harold Wax took his accordion. In some wards the musician were so moved that they could barely play. Sometimes only Shaw could sustain a full program playing solo.

After two months, they were moved to be nearer to an active combat zone in Espiritu Santo, the Northern most islands in the New Heberdes

Again Shaw luck played him low with out high rank; Shaw had no say so about the welfare of his men. Up here in a life or death zone, jazz music meant nothing. Shaw was treated badly.

Shaw had orders to play for the men for Navy morale, but no where had quarters been arranged for him and his men.

Shaw commented later in his book:

"I was the lowest of the low. The brass considered our mission to play concerts, silly! And I heard a lot of officers saying, "You're not in Hollywood now."

Shaw the Crown Prince of Jazz, the elite, the finest of the finest, put on his, combat face, and became a champion scrounger. He found bunks, bed clothes, food and water (always in short supply) for his men. He traded music for comforts.

And Shaw doggedly played concerts all over the area whether he was asked or not.

It paid off Shaw again.

"We'd set up in a clearing, Palm trees, a pounding surf, mountains in the distance, a damned Hollywood set. Marines, Seabees, Army guys would come crawling out of the bush sitting on the ground before the band and we'd crank up."

We'd be blasting, "Traffic Jam" or the "Back Bay Shuffle" and you could hardly hear yourself play, and as you looked at the grimy upturned faces you could see tears streaming down.

And, in moments such as this, it would strengthen our resolve. Damned straight! We would play whether they wanted us or not."

His treatment was erratic. On one island he would be deluged with gifts. Food, bottles of booze, an electric fan, and offers of help to expedite them on their way. On other islands there would be refused to use of jeeps and transportation, and not invited into Mess Halls. Shaw, without rank was helpless and bitter.

"I'll bet Glenn Miller never gets treated like this!" Shaw mused.

What bugged Shaw most of were low-grade officers who had a "Who do you think you are? Chip on their shoulders.

Shaw and his men were not unaware that their lives were on the line. On one trip to a neighboring island the Navy threw the off an Air Transport DC 3, and they were forced on a small ship. They were second in line. The first ship was torpedoed and all hands on board died. Things are getting tough. The band played on.

Shaw never had disciplinary problems. First of all, he was the master musician of them all. He kept his distance because he had to maintain the line, but all knew him as a friend outside the bandstand.

His biggest problem was Dave Tough. He was a very funny, dear man, who like all alcoholics, was always finding alcohol. When big dates came up, like a concert on an aircraft carrier Shaw would assign a man to stay with him 24 hours a day. Shaw loved the little guy, and highly evaluated his talent: Shaw said:

"I think he was the most underrated Big Band drummer in jazz, and he got a beautiful sound from his instrument. He tuned his drums, he tried to achieve on them what he heard in his head, as we all do, and he came as close as you can get. Tough refused to take solos. Whenever I pointed to him to take 12 or 8 or 4 bars, he'd smile and shake his head and go on playing those brilliant drums.

You couldn't stay mad at the little guy. He'd be playing the most knockout drums, kicking the band, a little smile on his face, and suddenly he'd fall off the bandstand, and he'd scramble back barely missing a beat with an apologetic smile on his face. How could you get mad at him?"

As they inched closer to the main islands of Japan they got better and better radio reception and Shaw enjoyed hearing all of his records played nightly. While they were on Guadalcanal word on the Tokyo radio came through that Shaw's wife had given birth to Steve, a healthy baby boy. There was a wild celebration that night despite the fact that it took place amid the whine and roar of Jap bombs.

On Guadalcanal the fighting was tough and unceasing. The band was beginning to break down physically. Their instruments fell apart. Dave Tough, already fragile, came down with Dengue Fever.

Even their intrepid leader began to show cracks.

One night he found himself walking down a dust road when he suddenly went blank.

"Where you going, Chief," said an officer in a passing jeep.

"I don't know," said Shaw, who drew a blank.

"Get in" said the officer quietly, recognizing the symptoms of combat fatigue. Shaw got in the jeep and bursts into uncontrollable tears.

Shaw couldn't stop crying in the hospital. "I probably would have been all right if the officer hadn't been so damned kind."

Beside the disintegration of the band's health and morale the hundred degree heat had a terrible effect on their instruments. Shaw again:

"I found it not unusual to be playing a solo and have a pad drop right out! Saltwater is murder on instruments. Reeds are impossible to get. The guitar and bass never could keep enough strings we were a mess!"

Shaw's health was permanently affected one night as he was caught in an air raid and jumped into a slit trench. Bombs went off on either side of him. The resultant concussion blew out his ear drums and he remained deaf for life from his left ear.

For the rest of that year they caught a break. There were booked up and down Australia, and then another few months in New Zealand. There were overwhelmed by their reception, but they had reached the end of the road.

Shaw had to admit they could progress no further.

"At that point the whole outfit was badly falling apart. By then our instruments were held together by rubber bands and sheer willpower, having survived any number of air raids, strafing runs, and long nights in damp foxholes; and the men themselves were in a state of dilapidation. That was it! We'd had it. The Navy Medical Board ordered us home."

Happy as they were, they found that they were expected to man the guns. Kaminsky said he was so weak he couldn't lift the shell, and had to recruit Dave to help lift the shells.

To keep their spirits up Kaminsky brought his horn, opened the speaker system, put in a mute, and played music all night.

They disembarked in San Francisco on November 11, 1943. Shaw was admitted to the Navy hospital at Oak Knoll, California. The official diagnosis: combat fatigue, migraine headaches, severe, deeply depressed, and he drifted into psychotic stupor.

Artie Shaw had served his country well. Now, he was through, finished. His war was over; now for the peace.

# Post War With Strings

After a lengthy hospital stay, Shaw jumped back into the band business with a big band of excellent L.A. musicians. The band featured a string section and used the basic book of the 41-42 bands.

After a shake out tour Shaw went into the studio for its first postwar recording session. He did two pop tunes Johnny Mercer's "Ac-cen-tuate the Positive" and "Let's Take a Long Way Home," and two excellent jazz oriented instrumentals, Jimmy Mundy's "Lady Day" and Ray Coniff's "Jumping on the Merry-go Round" Shaw liked for his composers to do the arranging and in this first date he succeeded.

The band was an immediate hit, and the tour was filled. The record company ordered him back to record. Again, he scored well. Two popular standards arranged by Ray Coniff: "I'll Never Be the Same" and a big hit "S'wonderful."

The surprise hit was by the newly formed Gramercy 5, which was now comprised of the brilliant Roy Eldridge a trumpet star, an 18 year old Dodo Marmarosa, and 20 year old Barney Kessel on guitar. Shaw showed his advanced ideas of jazz predating the bebop movement, keeping in tune with the advanced musical thinking Dodo and Kessel. Coupled with spectacular soloist and the dynamic punch and infectious swing of their performances the classical status of the two Shaw originals, "The Grabtown Grapple" (Grab Town was Ava Gardner's home) and "The Sad Sack" was guaranteed.

During the shake-out year Shaw fought RCA chief Eli Oberstein to make longer records. He was only allowed one 10 inch disc but it was a corker. Shaw recorded "Maid with a Flaccid Air" by Eddie Sauter, which approached the aura of some Shaw's prewar, pre Third Stream experiments. The other record was a superb Eddie Sauter arrangement of "Summertime" from Gershwin's Porgy and Bess. Critics felt it was the best recording of that lilting lullaby by any orchestra.

One more important thing occurred to wind up the year. Artie Shaw found Ava Gardner, and married her October 17, 1945. She lasted almost a year and they were divorced in September, 1946.

Shaw, ever the ladies' man, decided he had enough of movie actresses, and required higher intellectual woman, divorced Ava and promptly married Kathleen Windsor, a feisty and combative woman. She was the author of "Forever Amber" a huge best seller. Another marital war loomed on the horizon as they moved into a house in Norwalk, Connecticut. Shaw withdrew from music, and devoted himself to writing books, and arguing daily with Windsor.

The Shaw- Kathleen Windsor epic battles terminated in divorce in December, 1948.

Free once again, Shaw turned to long hair music. For the remainder of that year Shaw scheduled a series of long hair concerts playing a selection of Mozart for strings and clarinet. He toured for a year successfully, but found long hair music stifling and constricting. He missed the freedom of jazz.

He recorded with music craft, specifically a Cole Porter album. Interspersed in with his long hair concerts, Shaw formed various temporary bands and made money.

Decca appeared with a lucrative offer in 1950. They had already signed Ella Fitzgerald, Louis Armstrong, Coleman Hawkins, and Billie Holiday. But, instead of putting Shaw with the jazz giants, they assigned him pops singers such as Dick Haymes, Don Cherry, and vocal groups such as Gordon Jenkins choir, and even had Shaw record Christmas carols.

The time with Decca was painful and professional failure. He bought a diary farm, put down his clarinet, and started to write. In 1953 his book "The Trouble with Cinderella) came out and was well received. On June 29, 1952 Shaw unused to the single life, came up with a wealthy, but highly neurotic Doris Dowling. They had a child, on July 4, 1953. They named him Jonathan.

# The End of a Musical Road
# The Gramacy 5, 1953-54

By 1953 Shaw was at the end of his tether. He was heading toward a total dead end, and he sought to go out on a high note and not just run down.

He was offered eight weeks at the Embers, a top jazz joint in New York if he would reform the top Gramercy 5, with new material, as well as a smattering of old Shaw standards.

Emboldened by one last shot which would solve money problems and reach new critical heights, Shaw set out to hire the best of the new avant-garde musicians in the progressive jazz movement.

The initial Gramercy 5 was a blue-ribbon group of the best young musicians. On drums he hired Denzil Best who had played with George Shearing. On guitar Tal Farlow, Joe Rowland on vibes, and the famous Hank Jones on piano who was mainly a soloist, and an accompanist for Shaw's clarinet. The sound was original, new and highly successful.

On opening night Shaw still maintained his fructuous personality. Shaw looked out at the sold out crowd, and refused to go play the first set! Farlow grabbed him and asked what was the matter.

"Look at them! 80 percent are young women. They aren't here to hear us. They're here to see the **Shaw Thing**."

Perhaps he was right, but he had to go out and play. He needed the money. And the critics raved about the new group. The eight weeks was packed and the money flowed in.

Tal Farlow told me, "Slowly Shaw caved in to the public demand that he play the old swing pieces like he did in the old days. He fired Denzel Best, who was like our back bone, and brought in Irv Kluger, who had been Shaw's drummer for years. Unfortunately Kluger was an excellent big band swing drummer and did not fit in with the young progressive musicians. Since their contract specified that as long as Shaw played the new book, the young famous musicians would get scale pay. If Shaw faltered and slid back to swing they would get their "star" pay. Trouble brewed up fast.

The management wanted eight more weeks. Farlow was appointed to negotiate with Shaw. He found him in the dressing room, reading the New York Times and put the proposal of pay to Shaw. Shaw remained silent, reading the paper until he unfinished the column and then he put the paper down and said one word in answer to the band's request:

"Goodbye" said Shaw, put on his hat and left. Tal says he never saw or heard from him again.

Thus ended what could have given Shaw a money making second career.

Fortunately, for Shaw fans, Shaw liked his new music so much that he decided to record them at his own expense! The sides were recorded at the Fine Studios in the NBC building at 711 Fifth Avenue.

Artie Shaw said:

"The group sounded so good to me that I thought they should be recorded. After we finished work at 4:00 a.m. I would take the group to the studio, where we recorded the whole book! We were tired, but relaxed. Some sessions we'd finish at 10 or 11 in the morning."

This rare collection has been released again and again by different labels, and always selling well.

The remainder of the year sputtered from one booking to another, evoking critical praise, and paying his IRS debt.

His final appearance as a musician was an unmitigated disaster. Two American promoters in Australia decided to take $100,000 dollar gamble and signed up for a variety of jazz greats for concerts in Melbourne, Brisbane, and Sydney. The talent included Ella Fitzgerald, Buddy Rich, Artie Shaw and the famous comic Jerry Colonna.

The tour was a success, taking in $110,000 for seven days, but it was one of the most miserable experiences in Shaw's musical life. "The band was locals, who never heard my band, and they were unrehearsed, couldn't even play my theme or anything. They didn't know what a down beat was. It was hopeless. I tried to get drunk, but not even that worked. I lasted about seven days of agony, collected my pay, and came home my tail between my legs."

"That gig was the last I ever played in my life."

And so, Artie Shaw's professional life had ended.

# The Ride Out 1950's to 2005

Artie Shaw put down his clarinet at the age of 34. He never picked it up again. Ever

"Not even for the fun of it? Asked a British journalist.

"What makes you think that blowing into a block of wood, and using your lips, tongue and pharynx, and using tired lungs with your fingertips nimble enough to respond to the trigger sharp reflexes issued by the brain: what ever makes you think that is fun?"

It boggles the mind to think that Shaw could totally cut himself off from a lifetime habit of playing the clarinet.

At a young age he had arrived at the top of his field, and then he quit! Never to come back. Astonishing.

Artie managed to pick up one more wife, his eighth, Evelyn Keyes, Scarlet O'Hara's sister, went to live in Spain and came back and divorced her too.

He lived to the age of 94, dying peacefully in his sleep in a beautiful, commodious house on the side of a mountain, alone with his writing and memoirs. His band lives on today as an imitation road band with a good clarinetist playing Shaw's part, but let's face it, the Artie Shaw band <u>ain't</u> without Artie Shaw.

# About the Author: F. Pacheco M.D.

Ferdie Pacheco, MD has been called a Renaissance Man because of his polifacetic career. He has been successful as a pharmacist, medical doctor, Fight Doctor in boxing, including working as a corner man for twelve world champions, including Muhammed Ali for seventeen years. He also served as a boxing commentator for NBC, Showtime and Univision, winning two Emmies. During this time he was the Boxing Consultant for NBC for ten years. He is retired from broadcasting after being on for 25 years. He has had 14 books published, and written articles, columns, reviews for many of the major newspapers in America. He is a world recognized fine painter, and has recently focused on Florida history, specializing in Ybor City where he was born of Spanish parents.

Pacheco was seeing operations and autopsies as a child and at the same time he started to paint. Pacheco helped finance his medical education by contributing his cartoons to major national magazines.

He has been exhibiting his work in galleries since 1983. The awards for his art include Gold Medal and First Prize in Tonneins, France, Best Colorist at Musee du Luxembourg in Paris. Hi paintings are in the collections of many leading personalities in the world such as, Andy Garcia, Shirley MacLaine, Budd Schulberg, Petula Clark, Ernest Borgnine to name a few.

As a screenwriter he sold six scripts to major studios including Warners, Alan Ladd, King Hitzig, Paul Mazlansky, Canon Productions, and Salvatore Alabiso Productions.

For one year Pacheco appeared as a movie and book critic for CNBC-TV, as well as hosted a talk show segment.

He is an accomplished speaker and was under contract with Pinch Scotch for two years to speak every month on a series of subjects: boxing, art, books, history, and Flamenco dance.

He appeared as an actor, playing himself, in the movie "The Great White Hype." A movie he wrote for an Italian Company Pico Productions called "Virtually Yours" has been distributed throughout

Europe. A documentary on his life Ferdie Pacheco "The World of the Fight Doctor" will be shown on Public TV in the summer of 2004.

Pacheco is currently writing a volume of boxing stories of the famous 5th Street Gym.

Ferdie Pacheco has been happily married for 35 years to Luisita Sevilla, noted Flamenco artist and photographer, who also manages his art and types his manuscripts. They live in Miami.

# Books by Ferdie Pacheco:

| Title | Publisher | Year |
|---|---|---|
| Fight Doctor | Simon and Schuster | 1976, 1977 |
| Fight Doctor | Stanley Paul London | 1976, 78, 79 |
| Muhammad Ali a View from the Corner | Carol Publishing | 1992 |
| Renegade Lightning | Presidio Press | 1992 |
| Ybor City Chronicles | University Press of Florida | 1994-2004 |
| Columbia Restaurant Cook Book | University Press of Florida | 1995-2004 |
| Pacheco's Art of Ybor City | University Press of Florida | 1997-2004 |
| Christmas Eve Cookbook | University Press of Florida | 1998-2004 |
| Pacheco's Art of Cubans in Exile | Avanti Press | 2000 |
| The 12 Greatest Rounds of Boxing | Total Sports Publishing | 2000 |
| Trolley Kat | Hillsborough Press | 2001 |
| Trolley Kat ABC | Hillsborough Press | 2001 |
| The 12 Greatest Rounds of Boxing | Sports Media Publishing Canada | 2003 |
| Patton and the Mountain Man | Author House Publisher | 2004 |
| Blood in My Coffee | Sports Publications | 2004 |

T.V.:       25 years experience. NBC- Olympic Boxing, Seoul 88, Barcelona 92
            Univision-Spanish Cable: Boxing in Spanish, Showtime
Theater:    "Someone Like You" Original Story by for Petula Clark
Movies:     "Sweet Sam"Chanan Sazz/Cannon Globus
            "Night Lights" Alan King/ Hitzig Prod.,
            Alan Ladd Jr./Warners Paul Mazlansky Prod.
            "Liza" Liza Productions
            "Blue" Alabiso Prod.
            "The Spirit is Willing" Alabiso Prod./"Journeys" Rewrite

For more information go to: ferdiepacheco.com

Printed in the United States
42439LVS00005B/156

9 781420 838046